THE WI BOOK OF
BREAD
AND BUNS

MARY NORWAK

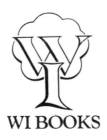

WI BOOKS

ACKNOWLEDGEMENTS

Illustrated by Cooper-West Graphic Design
Edited by Sue Jacquemier and Rosemary Wadey
Designed by Clare Clements
Cover photography by John Lee

Published by WI Books Ltd.,
39, Eccleston Street,
London SW1W 9NT

British Library Cataloguing in Publication Data
Norwak, Mary
   The WI book of bread and buns.
   1. Bread
   I. Title
   641.8'15   TX769

   ISBN 0-900556-82-X

First impression 1984

© Copyright 1984 by WI Books Ltd.

Filmset by
D. P. Media Limited, Hitchin, Hertfordshire

Reproduced, printed and bound in Great Britain by
Hazell Watson & Viney Limited,
Member of the BPCC Group,
Aylesbury, Bucks

CONTENTS

INTRODUCTION

Breadmaking is not difficult, but it is very important to understand the ingredients involved, and one or two basic preparation rules. Yeast cookery is very economical, since only small quantities of sugar and fat are used, and it is therefore appealing to many cooks. Amateurs, however, think that yeast is difficult to handle, and that too much time has to be spent in the various processes. In fact, there need be no problems when dealing with yeast, and actual work on the dough takes little time, and may easily be fitted in with other cooking or household tasks. Traditionally, country housewives used to bake bread on washing-day, because they knew they would be around the house all day, and the warm moist temperature was ideal for bread preparation.

How to use this book
This book is organised into five chapters. Basic recipes, which are referred to later in the chapter or elsewhere in the book, are positioned at the beginning of chapters.

Equipment
Special equipment is not necessary for yeast cookery. A large mixing bowl is important to hold the expanding dough – preferably an earthenware one (an old china washing bowl is ideal) but a polythene washing-up bowl kept specially for the purpose may be used. A measuring jug is useful for preparing yeast liquid. A large wooden spoon is best for mixing the dough before kneading. To speed up kneading, a dough hook fitted to an electric mixer is very effective, as well as saving a lot of time.

Bread and buns may be shaped and baked on thick baking sheets, or put into loaf tins which are usually available in 450-g (1-lb) and 900-g (2-lb) sizes. Cake tins may be used to shape bread if preferred. Clay loaf dishes are sometimes available and give a very good result and flavour, or clay flowerpots may be used (see page 32).

All equipment should be kept clean and dry. It is best to keep tins for bread-making only, and for preference they should not be washed but only wiped dry and clean. Lard or oil should be used for greasing containers.

Ingredients

Yeast is a raising agent which has been used for thousands of years, and it was the only means of raising bread and cakes until the 19th century. Brewer's yeast, autolysed and tonic yeast are not suitable for baking. Fresh yeast looks rather like putty, and may be bought at some bakers and health food stores. It should be creamy in colour, cool to the touch and easy to break. Yeast will keep fresh if tied in a polythene bag and stored in a cold place for five days (or one month in a refrigerator, or up to six months in a freezer).

Dried yeast is available in cans or 25-g (1-oz) packets from grocers, chemists and health food stores. It will keep up to six months if kept in an airtight container in a cool place, but will deteriorate quickly if there is a lot of air space in the can, and will not remain active.

When using dried yeast, only half the quantity is needed, compared to the amount of fresh yeast. In general, 25 g (1 oz) fresh yeast or 15 g (½ oz) dried yeast should be used with 1.5 kg (3 lb) white flour, but extra yeast is needed for wholemeal flour and for enriched mixtures.

Fresh yeast was traditionally creamed with a little sugar before adding to warm liquid, as sugar is a food for the yeast cells. Too much sugar tends to kill some of the yeast cells and produces the strong yeasty flavour which some people dislike in homemade bread. A little sugar in the warm liquid does however help to speed up the action of the yeast. When using dried yeast, it is important to remember that it should be frothing strongly in the warm liquid before being added to the flour.

There is also a new form of yeast called Easy Blend Dried Yeast, available in sealed packets. This is easy to use as it is stirred directly into the dry ingredients before liquid is added. It is very important to follow the manufacturer's instructions on the packet, and not to use this like ordinary dried yeast as this new variety will not work properly if added to liquid first.

Flour is available in many varieties for bread-making. Bread flour is made from strong hard wheat, and this strong flour absorbs more liquid than soft cake flours, and develops quickly with kneading into a firm elastic dough which gives a large volume and light texture. Strong flour (which is more glutinous than soft flour) also develops a stronger cell structure which supports the rising bread. White flour for breadmaking is labelled on the packet as 'strong flour' or 'bread flour'.

Wholemeal flour contains all the wheatgrain with nothing added or taken away and is described as 100% extraction flour, and has greater fibre content than white flour because it contains bran. Wheatmeal or brown flour contains 80–90% of the cleaned wheatgrain, with more bran than white flour. Wheatgerm flour has up to 10% extra wheatgerm added. Granary flour contains added bran and wheatgrains. Stoneground flour is produced by the traditional method of grinding between two horizontal stones, but most flour is now produced by the more modern method of roller milling.

Other grains such as rye, barley and oats were traditional bread ingredients, often grown in areas where wheat did not grow well. Rye is still used in Europe, and produced a slightly tough sour-tasting bread which is very good with meat, fish or cheese. Barley and oats are not suitable for yeast-raised breads, but may be raised with baking powder or bicarbonate of soda for griddle breads.

Some grocers stock bread flour, but the greatest variety of flours is generally found in health food stores. Some mills produce individual flours which may be bought in bulk.

Fat enriches dough, increases loaf volume, improves the softness and colour of the bread, and helps to delay the staling. If fat is melted before adding to a recipe, it should be cooled first but still flowing. Lard is generally used for plain bread, and butter for richer doughs.

Sugar is a food for yeast, but too much can kill off yeast cells and cause a yeasty flavour. Brown sugar gives a good flavour to wholemeal bread, or a little honey may be used.

Salt is essential to give flavour to yeast doughs, and bread without salt is quite unpleasant to eat. It helps prevent the yeast working too quickly, but too much will kill the yeast.

Liquid is needed to help the yeast work and to make a workable dough. Water, milk or a mixture may be used, generally allowing about 300 ml (½ pint) liquid to 450 g (1 lb) flour. All the liquid should be added at once to flour, and then a little extra flour or liquid may be needed to make a firm but soft dough. Different flours have different absorption rates, and wholemeal flour generally soaks up more liquid, but only experience tells a baker exactly how much liquid is needed for any individual flour.

Methods of using yeast

There are three ways of introducing the yeast to the flour in a recipe: (a) the liquid method, (b) the sponge batter method, and (c) rubbing in.

The liquid method is most commonly used for breadmaking. Fresh yeast should be mixed with lukewarm liquid and a little sugar. Dried yeast should be sprinkled on the lukewarm liquid with a little sugar and left in a warm place for about 10 minutes until frothy. A higher temperature is needed to start dried yeast (43°C/110°F).

The sponge batter is used for rich yeast mixtures. The fresh or dried yeast is added to the warm liquid with a little sugar and about one-third of the flour in the recipe. This forms a creamy paste which must be left in a warm place for about 20 minutes until it froths up like a sponge.

Rubbing in is sometimes used for soft doughs and yeast cakes. Fresh yeast is rubbed in like fat, but need not be broken up completely before the warm liquid is added. These mixtures must be beaten well to distribute the yeast evenly. If frozen yeast is used, it may be grated into the flour and will quickly start to work when warm liquid is used.

Temperature

Warmth is essential to good breadmaking. The mixing bowl should be warm when the flour is placed in it. A warm, slightly humid kitchen will produce good results, and draughts should be avoided. Contrary to old wives' tales, cold does not kill off yeast, and doughs may be allowed to rise slowly in a cool place, or even in the refrigerator. Risen dough may also be frozen for future use, but has to be returned to a warm room temperature so that the yeast continues working, and this does give the baker greater flexibility in timing the baking of doughs.

Liquid used in yeast bakery is generally described as lukewarm. As a quick guide to the correct temperature, use two-thirds hot liquid to one-third cold. The working of the yeast is finally finished when it is submitted to a hot oven temperature.

Kneading

Dough must be kneaded after mixing to give a good rise and an even crumb texture from the well-distributed yeast. It is important to allow plenty of time for kneading, which takes about 10 minutes by hand. To knead successfully, put the dough on a lightly floured board, and fold the dough, with the fingers together. Fold towards yourself, then push down and away with the ball of the hand. Give the dough a quarter-turn and keep kneading, developing a rocking rhythm. This can be done with one or both hands, and the action should not be delicate, but firm and decisive. The dough gradually changes until it feels smooth, firm, elastic and satiny, and is no longer sticky.

To speed up the kneading process, a dough hook on an electric mixer may be used, and the process then will take only 2–3 minutes. The dry ingredients and yeast liquid may be mixed with the dough hook on low speed, and then the speed increased slightly to knead the dough. The dough hook may also be used for the secondary kneading.

Rising (or 'proving')

Dough must rise at least once during preparation before baking so that the yeast works. The dough must be covered so that no skin forms on the surface. Traditionally, the dough was covered with a damp cloth, but may be placed in a large saucepan with a lid, or tied into an oiled polythene bag, leaving expansion space. The dough should double in size and will spring back when pressed gently with a floured finger.

General guidance is given for rising times in this book, but these will vary in different temperatures. A warm place gives a quick rise and refrigerator a slow one. A slow rise can give better results because it controls yeast growth: the dough rises evenly. Richer doughs take longer to rise then plain ones, and are easier to handle if given a cool rise.

Dough will rise in 45–60 minutes in a warm place, but will take 1½–2 hours at normal room temperature (21°C/75°F). It will need 8–12 hours to rise in a cold room or larder and up to 24 hours in a refrigerator. This means that a dough may be 'held back' overnight, then returned to room temperature for shaping and baking the next day. Dough should not be allowed to get too hot (e.g. placing near a hot solid-fuel cooker) as this will give a coarse, breakable crumb of irregular texture.

If the dough does not rise for long enough, the result will be a heavy, soggy loaf with a crust which breaks away from the top. If the dough rises for too long, the bread will lose its strength, colour, scent and flavour. A firm, soft dough gives the best results, as the yeast can work through the mixture, and if the dough is too stiff it will not expand.

Second rising

When dough has risen once, it must be 'knocked back' by flattening with the knuckles to knock out air bubbles and to give a better rise and even texture. The bread should then be kneaded quickly again for a minute or two in order to make the dough firm enough for baking.

Some doughs (e.g. pizza) are baked without a second rising, but most yeast breads should be shaped and placed in containers or on baking sheets before being covered and left for 20–45 minutes according to size, so that the dough rises again and becomes light and puffy. Free-shaped dough, as for buns, will double in size; dough in tins should rise to the rims. Use a sheet of lightly oiled polythene or a damp cloth to cover the dough.

Baking

Heat the oven before baking. Plain white and wholemeal doughs are generally baked at 230°C (450°F) mark 8. Enriched breads are baked at 190–220°C (375–425°F) mark 5–7.

When cooked, loaves shrink slightly from the sides of their containers and sound hollow when tapped underneath with the knuckles. If the sides of the bread are soft and pale when the given baking time is finished, the bread may be baked a little longer, but this can result in a very dark top crust. It is better to turn out the loaves and place them on their sides on the oven rack for about 5 minutes longer so that the sides become crisper and more golden.

Finishing

If a container of water is placed at the bottom of the oven, this will give the bread a crisper crust. Bread may be brushed with lightly salted water and sprinkled with cracked wheat, poppyseeds, caraway seeds, or sesame seeds before baking to give an attractive and slightly crunchy finish.

Enriched breads are often brushed with an egg wash of beaten egg with a little sugar and water before baking, to give an even golden shine to the finished loaf. Fruit breads and buns may be brushed with a little milk or beaten egg before baking to give a golden finish, and they are then given a sticky finish with a glaze of milk or water and sugar after baking. A quick shiny finish may be given by brushing the hot bread with a wet brush dipped in liquid honey.

Using a griddle

A griddle (or 'girdle') is a thick iron plate on a long handle, or with a loop handle, which may be used over a radiant ring or cooker hotplate for cooking some breads and scones. If a griddle is not available, a thick, heavy, flat frying pan may be used. It is best to heat the griddle until smoking hot, then lower the heat for cooking. The old rule for preparing the griddle was 'flour for dough and grease for batter'. Inexperienced cooks may find it difficult to use a lightly floured griddle without burning, and the surface may be very lightly greased with lard or oil instead, although the traditional floured surface of dough mixtures looks very attractive.

Food processors

A food processor may be used for preparing yeastless mixtures such as scones and gives excellent results if it is switched off as soon as the dough forms. When making yeast mixtures, it is also very important to switch off the machine as soon as a ball of dough forms. The bread will be heavy unless well kneaded by hand.

Quantities

Some of the recipes for basic breads may seem to yield a large number of loaves or rolls. In view of the time involved and the fuel used, it is seldom worth making a small quantity of yeast dough for an individual loaf or half a dozen rolls. Since yeast mixtures freeze exceptionally well, it is worth preparing a week's or month's supply at a time.

What went wrong?

It is important to follow recipe quantities for ingredients, and to follow methods carefully, but there can still be minor disasters, of which the following are the most common:

Coarse crumb and poor colour. Flour too soft; dough too firm; under- or over-proving (rising); insufficient salt.

Crumbly bread which stales quickly. Flour too soft; too much yeast; over-fermentation through rising too quickly in a very warm place.

Sour yeasty flavour. Too much yeast or stale yeast; too much sugar used to cream yeast; too long a fermentation (over-proving).

'Flying top' or cracked crust. Flour too soft; dough too firm; under-proving; too much dough for tin.

Poor volume with pale crust and flat top. Flour too soft; too little salt or yeast; insufficiently kneaded; proving temperature too high; over-proved; dough too wet or too dry.

Close heavy texture. Flour too soft; too much salt; insufficient kneading; under-proving; proving temperature too high; oven too cool.

Uneven texture and holes. Too much liquid and/or salt; under-proving or over-proving; insufficient kneading after first rising; dough left uncovered during rising, causing hard skin which forms streaks when kneaded.

Measurements

All spoon measures in this book are level unless stated otherwise.

3 tsp = 1 tbsp
8 tbsp = 5 fl oz = 150 ml = ¼ pint

Eggs are size 2 or 3 unless stated otherwise.

When following these recipes please use either the metric measurements or the imperial; do not mix them and then all will be well.

When a recipe states '450 g (1 lb) dough' it means dough made using 450 g (1 lb) flour. It does not mean 450 g (1 lb) prepared dough.

Measurements for can sizes are approximate.

American equivalents

	Metric	Imperial	American
Butter, margarine	225 g	8 oz	1 cup
Flour	100 g	4 oz	1 cup
Currants	150 g	5 oz	1 cup
Sugar	200 g	7 oz	1 cup
Syrup	335 g	11½ oz	1 cup

An American pint is 16 fl oz compared with the imperial pint of 20 fl oz. A standard American cup measure is considered to hold 8 fl oz.

BREADS WITH YEAST

This chapter contains many well known recipes
for basic loaves, rolls, croissants and muffins
together with some more unusual and foreign
recipes which use a variety of different
types of flour. All the recipes in this chapter
include yeast.

WHITE BREAD

Makes four 450-g (1-lb) loaves or
  36 rolls

1.5 kg (3 lb) strong plain white flour
25 g (1 oz) salt
25 g (1 oz) lard
25 g (1 oz) fresh yeast or
    15 g (½ oz) dried yeast
1 tsp sugar
900 ml (1½ pints) warm water

Sieve the flour and salt into a bowl and rub
in the lard until the mixture resembles fine
breadcrumbs. Mix the fresh yeast and sugar
and add to the lukewarm water (or sprinkle
the dried yeast on the water with the sugar
and leave until frothy). Add to the flour and
mix to a firm dough.

Knead very thoroughly for 10 minutes
(2–3 minutes with a dough hook on an
electric mixer). The dough should feel firm
and elastic, but not sticky. Shape into a
round ball, put into a greased bowl, cover
and leave to prove for 1 hour.

Divide the dough into four pieces and
knead each piece thoroughly. Fold up each
piece of dough to fit a greased 450-g (1-lb)
loaf tin. Cover and leave to prove again for
about 1 hour or until the dough rises just to
the top of the tins. Heat the oven to 230°C
(450°F) mark 8. Bake for 30–40 minutes
until the loaves shrink slightly from the tins
and the crust is deep golden brown. The
baked loaves will sound hollow when
tapped on the base. Cool on a wire rack.

This dough may be made into four
plaited loaves or four baps if preferred. If
tins are not available, it will also make 36
rolls, each weighing 50 g (2 oz), which will
only need 20 minutes' proving and
20 minutes' baking.

RYE BREAD

Makes 2 loaves

300 g (10 oz) rye flour
300 g (10 oz) strong plain white
  flour
1 tsp salt
25 g (1 oz) fresh yeast or
  15 g (½ oz) dried yeast
1 tsp sugar
150 ml (¼ pint) warm water
150 ml (¼ pint) warm milk
1 tbsp black treacle
2 tsp cornflour to glaze
150 ml (¼ pint) boiling water to
  glaze

Mix together the flours and salt in a bowl. Mix the fresh yeast with the sugar and lukewarm water (or sprinkle the dried yeast on the water with the sugar and leave until frothy). Heat the milk and treacle together until lukewarm. Add the yeast liquid and milk to the flour and work together to a firm dough. Knead well, cover and leave to prove for 1½ hours.

Knead the dough again and shape into two round loaves. Place on a greased baking sheet, cover and leave to prove for 45 minutes. Heat the oven to 230°C (450°F) mark 8. Mix the cornflour with a little cold water and add 150 ml (¼ pint) boiling water. Brush the bread with this glaze. Bake for 30 minutes then glaze again. Reduce the temperature to 150°C (300°F) mark 2 and continue baking for another 15 minutes. Brush with the glaze and bake for 5 minutes. Cool on a wire rack.

WHOLEMEAL BREAD

Makes four 450-g (1-lb) loaves or
  4 round cobs

1.5 kg (3 lb) wholemeal bread flour
25 g (1 oz) salt
25 g (1 oz) caster or soft brown
  sugar
25 g (1 oz) lard
50 g (2 oz) fresh yeast or
  25 g (1 oz) dried yeast
900 ml (1½ pints) warm water

Mix together the flour and salt, then add the sugar, reserving 1 teaspoonful. Rub in the lard. Mix the fresh yeast with the reserved sugar and lukewarm water (or sprinkle the dried yeast on the water with the sugar and leave until frothy). Work into the flour to give a soft, scone-like dough. Knead well for 10 minutes (or 2–3 minutes with a dough hook on an electric mixer). Shape into a ball, put into a greased bowl, cover and leave to prove for 1 hour.

Knead the dough again and divide into four pieces. Shape to fit four 450-g (1-lb) loaf tins, or into cobs. Cover and leave to prove again for about 1 hour until the loaves rise just to the top of the tins. Heat the oven to 230°C (450°F) mark 8. Bake for 40 minutes. Turn out and cool on a wire rack.

If liked, the flavour of the bread may be enriched by using honey or light soft brown sugar instead of white sugar. A little malt extract will also enhance the flavour. For a lighter 'brown' loaf, use a mixture of wholemeal and white flours.

ENRICHED WHITE BREAD

Makes 2 plaits or 12 rolls

450 g (1 lb) strong plain white flour
1 tsp salt
15 g (½ oz) fresh yeast or
*   7 g (¼ oz) dried yeast*
1 tsp sugar
250 ml (8 fl oz) warm milk
50 g (2 oz) butter, softened
1 egg, beaten

Egg wash
1 egg
1 tbsp water
1 tsp sugar

Weigh out 100 g (4 oz) flour and keep on one side. Sieve the remaining flour and salt into a bowl. Add the fresh or dried yeast to the sugar, lukewarm milk and reserved flour and mix well to form a batter. Leave to stand for about 20 minutes in a warm place until frothing vigorously. Add to the flour with the butter and beaten egg, and mix well. The dough will be quite soft. Turn on to a lightly floured board and knead for 10 minutes (or 2–3 minutes with a dough hook on an electric mixer). Form into a ball and put into a bowl. Cover and leave to prove for 45 minutes.

Heat the oven to 190°C (375°F) mark 5. Knead the dough again and shape into two plaits or 12 rolls. Place on a lightly greased baking sheet. Make the egg wash by beating the egg with the water and sugar. Brush all over the surface of the dough. Cover and prove for 30 minutes. Bake loaves for 45 minutes, or rolls for 15 minutes, until the base sounds hollow when tapped. Cool on a wire rack.

This dough may be flavoured with dried fruit, nuts or grated orange rind, and may be decorated with icing when cold. If fruit is added, the dough will take longer to rise.

SHORT-TIME BREAD

Makes two 450-g (1-lb) loaves or 18 rolls

675 g (1½ lb) strong plain white flour
15 g (½ oz) salt
7 g (¼ oz) fresh yeast
425 ml (14 fl oz) warm water
one 25-mg tablet ascorbic acid

If a small amount of Vitamin C (ascorbic acid) is used in bread-making, it reduces the first rising period for plain doughs to 5 minutes, and for enriched doughs to 10 minutes. Ascorbic acid tablets are obtainable from chemists in 25 mg, 50 mg and 100 mg sizes. They are dissolved in the yeast liquid, and fresh yeast is best used, as little time is saved when using dried yeast. The temperature of the liquid is very important when using this method: 32–38°C (90–100°F) if the room is cool; 27–32°C (80–90°F) if the room is warm. The second proving after shaping will be about 45 minutes in a warm room temperature.

Mix the flour, salt and sugar together in a large bowl and rub in the lard. Blend the fresh yeast with the warm water (see temperature above) and ascorbic acid. Add to the flour, mixing with a wooden spoon. Work to a firm dough and knead well for 10 minutes (2–3 minutes with a dough hook on an electric mixer). Shape into a ball, place on a bowl, cover and leave to stand for 5 minutes.

Flatten the dough and fold into three with the seam underneath. Put into a greased 900-g (2-lb) loaf tin or two 450-g (1-lb) tins, or shape into 18 rolls weighing 50 g (2 oz) each. Cover and leave to prove for 45 minutes (rolls 20 minutes). Heat the oven to 230°C (450°F) mark 8. Bake for 35 minutes (rolls 15 minutes). Cool on a wire rack.

Variation
To make wholemeal short-time bread, prepare the dough and cook in the same way, but use 450 ml (¾ pint) water.

HARVEST FESTIVAL BREAD

Makes one large design

1.5 kg (3 lb) strong plain white flour
1 tbsp salt
25 g (1 oz) fresh yeast or
15 g (½ oz) dried yeast
1 tsp sugar
900 ml (1½ pints) warm water
beaten egg to glaze
currants

Sieve the flour and salt together into a bowl. Mix the fresh yeast with the sugar and add to the lukewarm water (or sprinkle the dried yeast on the water with the sugar and leave until frothy). Add to the flour and mix to a firm dough. Knead well, shape into a ball, put into a greased bowl, cover and prove for 1½ hours.

Heat the oven to 220°C (425°F) mark 7. For a large design, the bread is modelled directly on to greased baking sheets that have been turned upside down so that the bread slides off easily when baked. Use two baking sheets side by side on an oven rack, which can then be lifted into place in the oven.

Loaves and Fishes design
Form half the dough into a large oval shape and roll out to about 2.5 cm (1 inch) thick. Place on the baking sheets. Use half the remaining dough and roll with the hands to a very long 'sausage' which will go completely around the edge of the oval. Twist to form a rope and fix around the edge of the oval with beaten egg. Make small flat fishes and tiny cottage loaves with the remaining dough. Arrange on the dough base. Brush the whole shape with beaten egg. Bake for 20 minutes, then reduce the temperature to 160°C (325°F) mark 3 and continue baking for 30 minutes.

Wheatsheaf design
Measure 225 g (8 oz) dough and form into a sausage shape 30 cm (12 inches) long. Place in the centre of the baking sheets and flatten slightly to form the base of the design. Take 350 g (12 oz) dough and form a crescent shape. Arrange at the top end of the

'sausage', flattening slightly. This is the shape of the wheatsheaf. Use half the remaining dough to shape thin 'sausages' the width of pencils and 30 cm (12 inches) long. Arrange on the basic stalk to cover completely. Plait three of these strands and arrange across the thin stalks like string, tucking under the ends.

Use 50 g (2 oz) dough to shape a mouse and thin tail. Arrange on the stems and add currants for eyes. Divide the remaining dough into 25-g (1-oz) pieces. Form into sausage shapes and arrange all over the crescent like sunrays. Clip each sausage shape two or three times with scissors to make V-shapes (these are the ears of corn). Brush the whole shape with beaten egg. Bake as for Loaves and Fishes.

These bread shapes are ideal for church festivals or harvest suppers, but are not usually eaten. They will keep for years if sprayed with artist's picture varnish, and make attractive decorations.

OAT LOAF

Makes 1 loaf

300 g (10 oz) strong plain white
   flour
175 g (6 oz) porridge oats
1 tsp salt
15 g (½ oz) fresh yeast or
   7 g (¼ oz) dried yeast
1 tsp sugar
150 ml (¼ pint) warm water
150 ml (¼ pint) warm milk
2 tsp salad oil
a little milk and oats to finish

Stir the flour and oats together with the salt in a bowl. Mix the fresh yeast and sugar and add to the lukewarm water (or sprinkle the dried yeast on the water with the sugar and leave until frothy). Add to the flour with the lukewarm milk and oil and mix to a soft dough. Knead well, cover and leave to prove for 1 hour. Knead again.

Heat the oven to 200°C (400°F) mark 6. Knead the dough again then divide into three pieces and roll into sausage shapes. Plait together and place on a greased baking sheet. Cover and leave to prove for 30 minutes. Brush with a little milk and sprinkle with a few oats. Bake for 30 minutes then cool on a wire rack.

FRENCH FLUTES

Makes 4 loaves

900 g (2 lb) strong plain white flour
25 g (1 oz) fresh yeast or
   15 g (½ oz) dried yeast
1 tsp sugar
600 ml (1 pint) water
15 g (½ oz) salt
milk or melted butter to glaze

Sieve half the flour into a bowl. Mix the fresh yeast with the sugar and add to half the lukewarm water (or sprinkle the dried yeast on half the water with the sugar and leave until frothy). Add to the flour and mix well. Cover and leave to prove for 3 hours. Warm the remaining water and add the salt. Pour over the dough (which will have a crusty skin on it) and mix until the skin disappears. Gradually work in the remaining flour and knead for 15 minutes.

Lift the dough and slap it down in the bowl, and keep repeating this process for 5 minutes. Cover and leave to prove for 2 hours.

Divide the dough into four portions and roll into balls. Place on a floured board, cover with a dry cloth, and leave for 15 minutes. Roll and pull each ball into a long sausage shape. Put the shapes on a cloth and pull the cloth tightly up the sides and between the loaves so that they do not expand sideways. Cover and leave to prove for 1 hour.

Heat the oven to 230°C (450°F) mark 8. Lift the loaves on to greased baking sheets and slash each loaf three times with a sharp knife. Bake for 30 minutes, turn the loaves and brush with milk or melted butter. Return to the oven for 10 minutes. Cool on a wire rack.

CHALLAH

Makes 1 loaf

450 g (1 lb) strong plain white flour
½ tsp salt
25 g (1 oz) fresh yeast or
    15 g (½ oz) dried yeast
1 tsp sugar
250 ml (8 fl oz) warm water
pinch of saffron
2 eggs, beaten
1 egg yolk to glaze

Sieve the flour and salt into a bowl. Mix the fresh yeast with the sugar and add to the lukewarm water (or sprinkle the dried yeast on the water with the sugar and leave until frothy). Soak the saffron in 1 tablespoon boiling water. Add the yeast to the flour with the saffron liquid and beaten eggs. Knead until smooth, cover and leave to prove for 1½ hours.

Knead the dough again and divide into three pieces. Roll into sausage shapes and plait together, tucking in the ends. The loaf should be high and well rounded. Place on a greased baking sheet, cover and leave to prove for 1 hour. Brush with the egg yolk. Heat the oven to 200°C (400°F) mark 6. Bake for 10 minutes, then reduce the temperature to 190°C (375°F) mark 5 and continue baking for 35 minutes. Cool on a wire rack.

This is a Jewish bread.

NAAN BREAD

Makes 12

675 g (1½ lb) self-raising flour
pinch of salt
450 ml (¾ pint) natural yoghurt
1 tsp fresh yeast or ½ tsp dried yeast
2 tbsp warm water
50 g (2 oz) melted butter

Sieve the flour into a bowl with the salt. Work in the yoghurt. Mix the yeast with warm water and leave for 5 minutes until it is frothy. Add to the flour, mix well and knead lightly. Cover and leave to stand for 24 hours. Divide the dough into 12 pieces and roll out each piece into a thin oval on a floured board. Put on a greased baking sheet and brush with melted butter. Grill under a high heat for 2 minutes on each side until brown. Serve warm.

This Indian bread is a traditional accompaniment to tandoori food. It should be flat, soft, moist inside, and slightly scorched on the outside.

KENT HUFFKINS

Makes 8

675 g (1½ lb) strong plain white
    flour
1½ tsp salt
50 g (2 oz) lard
15 g (½ oz) fresh yeast or
    7 g (¼ oz) dried yeast
1 tsp sugar
450 ml (¾ pint) warm milk and
    water

Sieve the flour and salt into a bowl and rub in the lard until the mixture resembles fine breadcrumbs. Mix the fresh yeast and sugar and add to the lukewarm milk and water (or sprinkle the dried yeast on the liquid with the sugar and leave until frothy). Add to the flour and mix to a soft dough. Knead, cover and leave to prove for 1 hour.

Heat the oven to 230°C (450°F) mark 8. Knead well and divide the mixture into eight pieces. Form each piece into a ball and roll out to 2.5 cm (1 inch) thick. Put on a greased baking sheet, cover and prove for 20 minutes. Press each piece of dough firmly in the centre with a floured thumb. Bake for 20 minutes, turning the huffkins over half-way through baking. Wrap in a clean tea towel while cooling so that they remain soft.

BAGELS

Makes 12

350 g (12 oz) strong plain white
flour
½ tsp salt
25 g (1 oz) fresh yeast or
15 g (½ oz) dried yeast
2 tsp sugar
150 ml (¼ pint) warm water
3 tbsp melted butter
1 egg, beaten
caraway seeds to decorate (optional)

Sieve the flour and salt into a bowl. Mix the yeast and sugar and add to the lukewarm water (or sprinkle the dried yeast on the water with the sugar and leave until frothy). Work into the flour with the melted butter and beaten egg. Knead to a smooth dough. Cover and leave to prove for 45 minutes.

Heat the oven to 200°C (400°F) mark 6. Knead the dough well for 5 minutes and divide into 12 pieces. Roll each into a 'sausage' about 20 cm (8 inches) long. Form into rings and press the edges together firmly. Sprinkle with caraway seeds, if liked. Put on a floured baking sheet and bake for 5 minutes.

Have ready a large pan of boiling water. Drop in the dough rings and boil for 20 minutes. Drain well and put back on the baking sheet. Bake for 15 minutes. Serve sliced horizontally and spread with butter or cream cheese.

These are a very good accompaniment to smoked fish.

DERBYSHIRE PIKELETS

Makes 12

225 g (8 oz) strong plain white flour
1 tsp salt
7 g (¼ oz) fresh yeast or
1 tsp dried yeast
1 tsp sugar
300 ml (½ pint) warm milk
1 egg, beaten

Sieve the flour and salt into a bowl. Mix the fresh yeast with the sugar and add to the lukewarm milk (or sprinkle the dried yeast on the milk with the sugar and leave until frothy). Add to the flour with the beaten egg and beat well to make a thin batter. Cover and leave to stand for 30 minutes.

Pour a small cupful of the batter on to a greased griddle or thick frying pan. Cook until one side is golden brown, then turn and cook until the underside is golden. Eat hot with butter.

BAPS

Makes 10

450 g (1 lb) strong plain white flour
1 tsp salt
50 g (2 oz) lard
2 tsp sugar
25 g (1 oz) fresh yeast or 15 g
    (½ oz) dried yeast
300 ml (½ pint) warm milk and
    water

Sieve the flour and salt into a bowl and rub in the lard until the mixture resembles fine breadcrumbs. Stir in half the sugar. Mix the fresh yeast with the remaining sugar and add to the lukewarm liquid (or sprinkle the dried yeast on the liquid with the sugar and leave until frothy). Add to the flour and work to a soft dough. Knead well, cover and prove for 1 hour.

Heat the oven to 230°C (450°F) mark 8. Knead the dough again and divide into ten pieces. Shape into small, flat loaves about 10 cm (4 inches) across. Place on a greased baking sheet, cover and prove for 20 minutes. Brush with a little milk or dredge with flour. Bake for 20 minutes. Wrap in a clean tea towel so that the baps remain soft while cooling.

BRIDGE ROLLS

Makes 12

450 g (1 lb) strong plain white flour
1 tsp salt
25 g (1 oz) fresh yeast or
    15 g (½ oz) dried yeast
2 tsp sugar
300 ml (½ pint) milk
25 g (1 oz) butter, melted
2 eggs
a little beaten egg to glaze

Sieve the flour and salt into a bowl. Mix the fresh yeast with the sugar and add to the lukewarm milk (or sprinkle the dried yeast on the milk with the sugar and leave until frothy). Add to the flour with the cooled butter and beaten eggs and mix to a soft dough. Knead lightly, cover and prove for 45 minutes.

Heat the oven to 230°C (450°F) mark 8. Knead the dough well and roll out to 1 cm (½ inch) thick. Cut into finger lengths and shape rounded ends. Put on to a greased baking sheet so that the rolls just touch. Cover and leave to prove for 15 minutes. Brush with beaten egg and bake for 15 minutes. Cool on a wire rack and pull apart when cold.

POPPY SEED ROLLS

Makes 15

450 g (1 lb) strong plain white flour
1 tsp salt
50 g (2 oz) butter or margarine
15 g (½ oz) fresh yeast or
    7 g (¼ oz) dried yeast
1 tsp sugar
300 ml (½ pint) warm milk
2 eggs, beaten
15 g (½ oz) poppy seeds

Sieve the flour and salt into a bowl. Rub in the fat until the mixture resembles fine breadcrumbs. Mix the fresh yeast with the sugar and add to the lukewarm milk (or sprinkle the dried yeast on the milk with the sugar and leave until frothy). Add to the flour with 1 beaten egg and mix well. Work to a soft dough and knead until smooth and elastic. Leave to prove for 30 minutes.

Heat the oven to 220°C (425°F) mark 7. Knead the dough again and then divide into 15 pieces. Shape into round rolls, miniature cottage loaves or plaited batons. Place on a greased baking sheet, cover and leave to prove for 15 minutes. Brush with the other beaten egg and sprinkle with poppy seeds. Bake for 20 minutes, then cool on a wire rack.

PAIN DE MIE

Makes one 900-g (2-lb) loaf

550 g (1¼ lb) strong plain white
    flour
1 tsp salt
50 g (2 oz) sugar
25 g (1 oz) fresh yeast or
    15 g (½ oz) dried yeast
300 ml (½ pint) warm water
100 g (4 oz) butter, softened
2 eggs

Sieve the flour and salt into a bowl. Stir in the sugar, reserving 1 teaspoonful. Mix the fresh yeast with the reserved sugar and add to the lukewarm water (or sprinkle the dried yeast on the water with the sugar and leave until frothy). Add the flour with the butter and eggs to make a soft, spongy dough. Knead well, cover and leave to prove for 1 hour.

Knead the dough again and shape to fit a greased 900-g (2-lb) loaf tin. Cover and leave to prove for 45 minutes. Heat the oven to 200°C (400°F) mark 6. Bake for 40 minutes then cool on a wire rack. This bread should retain a soft crust.

MUFFINS

Makes 8

450 g (1 lb) strong plain white flour
1 tsp salt
15 g (½ oz) fresh yeast or
    7 g (¼ oz) dried yeast
1 tsp sugar
300 ml (½ pint) warm water
flour or fine semolina to dredge

Sieve the flour and salt into a bowl. Mix the fresh yeast with the sugar and add to the lukewarm water (or sprinkle dried yeast on the water with the sugar and leave until frothy). Add to the flour and mix well. Knead to a firm dough. Cover and leave to prove for 1 hour. Knead lightly again and roll out on a floured board to 1 cm (½ inch) thickness. Cover and leave to stand for 5 minutes. Cut into 7.5-cm (3-inch) diameter rounds. Place on a well floured baking sheet and dredge the tops with flour or fine semolina (this gives a golden and slightly crisp finish). Cover and leave to prove for 40 minutes.

Heat the oven to 230°C (450°F) mark 8 or prepare a griddle. Cook on a moderately hot greased griddle or thick frying pan for about 6 minutes each side until golden brown *or* bake for 10 minutes, turning over after 5 minutes.

To serve, pull the muffins open all the way round, leaving the halves joined in the centre. Toast on both sides, then pull apart and butter thickly. Put together again and serve hot.

BRIOCHES

Makes 12

225 g (8 oz) strong plain white flour
½ tsp salt
15 g (½ oz) sugar
15 g (½ oz) fresh yeast or
    7 g (¼ oz) dried yeast
2 tbsp water
2 eggs, beaten
50 g (2 oz) butter, melted

Sieve the flour and salt into a bowl, and stir in the sugar, reserving 1 teaspoonful. Mix the fresh yeast and reserved sugar with the lukewarm water (or sprinkle dried yeast on the water with the sugar and leave until frothy). Add to the dough and mix in the beaten eggs and cooled butter. Work to a soft dough and knead well until smooth. Cover and leave to prove for 1½ hours.

Egg wash
1 egg
1 tbsp water
pinch of sugar

Heat the oven to 230°C (450°F) mark 8. Knead the dough again and divide into 12 pieces. Grease 12 brioche tins, or use castle pudding tins, or deep patty tins. Shape three-quarters of each piece of dough into a ball and put into the tins. Shape remaining dough pieces into small balls. With the finger, press a hole firmly in the centre of each large ball and place the smaller piece on top. Place the tins on a baking tray. Cover and leave to prove for 45 minutes. Mix all the ingredients for the egg wash, and brush over each brioche. Bake for 10 minutes. Turn out and cool on a wire rack. Serve freshly baked.

CRUMPETS

350 g (12 oz) strong plain white
  flour
15 g (½ oz) fresh yeast or
  7 g (¼ oz) dried yeast
1 tsp sugar
325 ml (11 fl oz) warm water
2 tsp salt
½ tsp bicarbonate of soda
150 ml (¼ pint) milk

Sieve the flour into a bowl. Mix the yeast with the sugar and lukewarm water and leave to stand for 5 minutes. Mix into the flour, cover and leave to prove for about 2 hours until very light and fluffy and about to collapse. Add the salt and soda to the milk and beat into the yeast batter so that the mixture is runny.

Lightly grease a hot griddle or thick frying pan and put four well-greased poaching rings on it. Pour batter into the rings to come half-way up the sides. Lower the heat and cook gently for 10 minutes until each crumpet is set. Turn over and cook for 2 minutes until golden brown. The poaching rings may be removed when the mixture is set, then greased ready for the next batch. Fresh crumpets may be eaten with butter while still hot, or they may be toasted on both sides before buttering.

RYE CRISPBREAD

Makes about 18

½ quantity risen rye bread dough
(see page 16)
2 tbsp oil
1 tsp salt
1 tbsp crushed cornflakes (or coarse
rye)
1 tsp caraway seeds (optional)

Heat the oven to 200°C (400°F) mark 6.
Work all the ingredients together until
thoroughly blended. Put on a lightly floured
board and roll out thinly. Cut into squares
or circles and place on a greased baking
sheet. Cover and leave to prove for about
15 minutes until puffy. Bake for
15 minutes. Turn off the oven and leave the
door slightly ajar. Remove bread from the
oven when cold and crisp. Store in an
airtight tin.

SWEDISH LIMPA

Makes 1 loaf

200 ml (7 fl oz) brown ale
1 tbsp vinegar
100 g (4 oz) black treacle
15 g (½ oz) caraway seeds
15 g (½ oz) fresh yeast, or
7 g (¼ oz) dried yeast and 1 tsp
caster sugar
225 g (8 oz) rye flour
225 g (8 oz) strong plain white flour
1 tsp salt
25 g (1 oz) lard

Put the ale, vinegar, black treacle and
caraway seeds into a pan and heat until
lukewarm. Crumble in the fresh yeast (if
using dried yeast, sprinkle on to
4 tablespoons lukewarm water with
1 teaspoon sugar and leave until frothy).
Add the frothing dried yeast to the warm ale
mixture. Mix the rye flour and white flour
in a bowl with the salt and rub in the lard.
Add the ale mixture and mix to a firm
dough. Knead well to give a smooth dough.
Cover and leave to prove for 2 hours.

Knead again and shape into a round loaf.
Place on a greased baking sheet, cover and
leave to prove for 1 hour. Heat the oven to
190°C (375°F) mark 5. Bake for
45 minutes. Cool on a wire rack.

AMERICAN SPOON BREAD

Makes one 900-g (2-lb) loaf

350 g (12 oz) wholemeal flour
225 g (8 oz) cornmeal
1 tsp salt
15 g (½ oz) fresh yeast or
  7 g (¼ oz) dried yeast
2 tbsp clear honey
250 ml (8 fl oz) warm water
250 ml (8 fl oz) warm milk
1 tbsp oil
1 egg, beaten

Stir the flour, cornmeal and salt together. Mix the fresh yeast and honey and add to the lukewarm water (or sprinkle the dried yeast on the water with the honey and leave until frothy). Add to the flour with the lukewarm milk, oil and beaten egg. Beat well, cover and leave to prove for 30 minutes.

Heat the oven to 180°C (350°F) mark 4. Stir the batter well and put into a greased 900-g (2-lb) loaf tin. Cover and leave to prove for 20 minutes then bake for 50 minutes.

Americans spoon this bread straight from the tin and eat it with butter as an accompaniment to a meal. The bread may also be turned out to cool on a wire rack, then sliced and buttered.

PITTA BREAD

Makes 6

675 g (1½ lb) risen white or
  wholemeal dough (see page 15 or
  16)
plain flour

Heat the oven to 220°C (425°F) mark 7. Knead the dough and divide into six even-sized pieces. Knead each piece into a ball on a lightly-floured board, and shape into a 20 x 10 cm (8 x 4 inch) oval. Dredge lightly with flour and fold in half by bringing the top over the bottom. Press edges together lightly to seal. Put on well-greased baking sheets and bake for 20 minutes.

Remove from the baking sheets and wrap each piece of bread loosely in foil so that it remains soft as it cools. The bread forms a 'pocket' into which salads, eggs, hot or cold meat or fish may be slipped, to form a convenient hand-held meal.

GRANARY BREAD

Makes 1 loaf

450 g (1 lb) granary flour
1 tsp salt
15 g (½ oz) fresh yeast or
7 g (¼ oz) dried yeast
1 tsp sugar
300 ml (½ pint) warm water
1 tbsp malt extract
1 tbsp salad oil
25 g (1 oz) cracked wheat

Mix the flour and salt in a bowl. Mix the fresh yeast with the sugar and add to the lukewarm water (or sprinkle the dried yeast on the water with the sugar and leave until frothy). Add to the flour with the malt extract and oil and mix well. Knead to a soft dough. Cover and leave to prove for 1 hour.

Heat the oven to 220°C (425°F) mark 7. Knead the dough again and shape into a round. Put on a greased baking sheet. Brush with a little water and sprinkle with the cracked wheat. Cover and leave to prove for 30 minutes. Bake for 35 minutes then cool on a wire rack.

FLOWERPOT LOAVES

Makes 2 loaves

225 g (8 oz) wholemeal bread flour
175 g (6 oz) strong plain white flour
2 tsp salt
25 g (1 oz) lard
15 g (½ oz) fresh yeast or
7 g (¼ oz) dried yeast
1 tsp sugar
300 ml (½ pint) warm water

Mix the flours and salt together in a bowl and rub in the lard. Mix the fresh yeast and sugar and add to the lukewarm water (or sprinkle the dried yeast on the water with the sugar and leave until frothy). Add to the flour and mix to a soft dough. Knead until smooth, shape into a ball, place in a bowl, cover and leave to prove for 1 hour.

Use new clay flowerpots. Grease them well with oil or lard and bake empty for 30 minutes in a hot oven before use to prevent breakage.

Heat the oven to 230°C (450°F) mark 8. Knead the dough again and divide into two pieces. Place in well-greased 12.5-cm (5-inch) clay flowerpots. Cover and leave to prove for 30 minutes. Stand the pots upright on a baking sheet, and bake for 35 minutes. Turn out carefully on to a wire rack to cool. Clean pots thoroughly, dry and reserve for future use.

CROISSANTS

Makes 12

450 g (1 lb) strong plain white flour
2 tsp salt
25 g (1 oz) lard
25 g (1 oz) fresh yeast or
    15 g (½ oz) dried yeast
1 tsp sugar
250 ml (8 fl oz) water
1 egg, beaten
175 g (6 oz) butter

Egg wash
1 egg
1 tbsp water
pinch of sugar

Sieve the flour and salt into a bowl and rub in the lard. Mix the fresh yeast and sugar with the lukewarm water (or sprinkle the dried yeast on the water with the sugar and leave until frothy). Add to the flour with the beaten egg and work to a soft dough. Knead well until smooth. Roll out the dough into a rectangle 50 x 20 cm (20 x 8 inches).

Soften the butter by mashing with a knife and divide into three portions. Dot one portion of butter over two-thirds of the dough. Fold the bottom third of dough upwards, then the top third downwards. Turn the dough so that the fold is on the right-hand side. Roll out the dough to the same size and repeat the process of dotting with butter, folding and rolling, twice more. In between the processes, wrap the dough and leave to rest in a cool place for 10 minutes each time. After the last folding, cover and leave in the refrigerator for 30 minutes.

Roll out to a rectangle, fold and roll again. Repeat this three times, then roll into a rectangle 55 x 33 cm (22 x 13 inches). Cover and leave to stand for 10 minutes. Trim the edges with a sharp knife to give a neat rectangle, then divide lengthwise into two rectangles. Cut each strip into six triangles with a 15-cm (6-inch) base. Make up egg wash by beating together the egg, water and sugar. Brush the triangles with egg wash and roll up loosely towards the point, finishing with the top underneath. Curve into crescent shapes.

Heat the oven to 220°C (425°F) mark 7. Place the croissants on lightly greased baking sheets, cover and prove for 30 minutes. Brush with egg wash. Bake for 15 minutes. Cool on a wire rack. Serve warm.

BUNS, TEACAKES AND PASTRIES

Buns and teacakes were traditional treats made
from simple bread dough slightly sweetened
and enriched with fat and dried fruit. In
Scandinavia, there is also a traditional of festive
bun-making, but many European countries
prefer more elaborate treats in the form of
yeast pastry with rich fillings, twisted into
intricate shapes.

OLD-FASHIONED CURRANT BUNS

Makes 12

Batter
100 g (4 oz) strong plain white flour
25 g (1 oz) fresh yeast or
   15 g (½ oz) dried yeast
1 tsp sugar
200 ml (7 fl oz) warm milk and
   water

Dough
350 g (12 oz) strong white plain
   flour
1 tsp salt
50 g (2 oz) butter or margarine
50 g (2 oz) sugar
100 g (4 oz) currants
1 egg, beaten

Glaze
50 g (2 oz) sugar
4 tbsp water

Prepare the batter first. Sieve the flour into a bowl. Mix the fresh yeast with the sugar and add to the lukewarm milk and water (or sprinkle the dried yeast on the liquid with the sugar and leave until frothy). Add the yeast liquid to the flour, mix well, cover and leave to stand for 30 minutes.

To make the dough: sieve the flour and salt into a bowl. Rub in the fat until the mixture resembles fine breadcrumbs. Stir in the sugar. Add the yeast liquid and mix to a soft dough. Knead well, cover and leave to prove for 1½ hours.

Heat the oven to 220°C (425°F) mark 7. Knead the dough again and work in the currants. Divide into twelve pieces and shape each one into a ball. Put on a lightly greased baking sheet and flatten slightly. Cover and leave to prove for 30 minutes. Brush with beaten egg and bake for 20 minutes.

To make the glaze, dissolve the sugar in the water and boil for 1 minute. While the buns are still warm, brush with this glaze. Cool on a wire rack.

ALMOND PASTE

50 g (2 oz) ground almonds
175 g (6 oz) icing sugar, sieved
1 egg white

Mix the ground almonds, icing sugar and egg white to a smooth paste, adding a little water if necessary.

GLACÉ ICING

225 g (8 oz) icing sugar
water

Mix sieved sugar with just enough cold water to give the necessary consistency. 1½-2 tablespoons water will give a soft pouring consistency, while 1 tablespoon water will give a thicker icing which can be spread on cakes or buns.

Lemon or orange juice may be substituted for water. A little cocoa or coffee essence may be added to give flavour, or the icing may be lightly coloured with a few drops of food colouring.

If a shiny icing is preferred, put the icing sugar and water into a small pan and stir over very low heat until well blended.

TEACAKES

Makes 3

225 g (8 oz) strong plain white flour
15 g (½ oz) butter
15 g (½ oz) fresh yeast or
   7 g (¼ oz) dried yeast
1 tsp sugar
150 ml (¼ pint) warm milk
1 egg, beaten
40 g (1½ oz) mixed dried fruit

Glaze
1 tbsp caster sugar
2 tbsp milk

Sieve the flour into a bowl and rub in the butter. Mix the fresh yeast with the sugar and add to the lukewarm milk (or sprinkle dried yeast on the milk with the sugar and leave until frothy). Add to the flour with the egg and dried fruit, mix thoroughly and knead well. Cover and leave to prove for 45 minutes.

Heat the oven to 230°C (450°F) mark 8. Knead the dough again on a floured board and divide into three pieces. Knead each piece until smooth and round, and then shape into a flat round cake. Put the three cakes on a greased baking sheet. Cover and leave to prove for 15 minutes. Bake for 12 minutes.

To glaze: dissolve the sugar in the milk by heating it and use to brush over the buns while they are still warm. Leave to cool on a wire rack.

PATELEY FRITTERS

Makes 18

450 g (1 lb) strong plain white flour
225 g (8 oz) sugar
50 g (2 oz) currants
50 g (2 oz) sultanas
pinch of salt
pinch of ground nutmeg
15 g (½ oz) fresh yeast or
    7 g (¼ oz) dried yeast
1 tsp sugar
pinch of pepper
150 ml (¼ pint) warm milk
1 egg, beaten

Sieve the flour into a bowl. Stir in the sugar, currants, sultanas, salt and nutmeg. Mix the fresh yeast with sugar and pepper and add to the lukewarm milk (or sprinkle dried yeast on the milk with the sugar and pepper and leave until frothy). Work into the dry ingredients with the egg, and beat into a smooth thick batter, adding a little more warm milk if necessary. Cover and leave to prove for 1 hour.

Grease a thick frying pan or griddle and drop tablespoons of the batter at intervals on the hot surface. Cook until golden brown underneath, then turn and cook the other side until golden brown.

These were traditionally eaten in the West Riding of Yorkshire on Ash Wednesday.

SWISS BUNS

Makes 12

Batter
100 g (4 oz) strong plain white flour
25 g (1 oz) fresh yeast or
    15 g (½ oz) dried yeast
1 tsp sugar
200 ml (7 fl oz) warm milk

Dough
350 g (12 oz) strong plain white
    flour
1 tsp salt
50 g (2 oz) lard
50 g (2 oz) sugar
1 egg, beaten

glacé icing (see page 36)

Prepare the batter and dough as for currant buns (see page 35). Heat the oven to 220°C (425°F) mark 7.

Knead the dough again and shape into 12.5-cm (5-inch) long finger shapes. Place on a lightly greased baking sheet, cover and leave to prove for 30 minutes. Bake for 20 minutes and cool on a wire rack. When cool, coat with glacé icing (see page 36).

BATH BUNS

Makes 12

450 g (1 lb) strong plain white flour
25 g (1 oz) fresh yeast or
    15 g (½ oz) dried yeast
1 tsp sugar
200 ml (7 fl oz) warm milk and
    water
1 tsp salt
50 g (2 oz) butter or margarine
75 g (3 oz) caster sugar
2 eggs, beaten
100 g (4 oz) sultanas
50 g (2 oz) chopped mixed peel
a little beaten egg
50 g (2 oz) cube sugar

Mix together 100 g (4 oz) of the flour, the yeast, 1 teaspoon sugar and the lukewarm liquid in a bowl. Cover and leave for 20 minutes until the batter is soft and spongy. Sieve the remaining flour with the salt into a large bowl and rub in the fat until the mixture resembles fine breadcrumbs. Stir in the caster sugar. Add this dry mixture to the yeast batter with the eggs, sultanas and peel. Mix well and then beat very thoroughly (the dough is too soft to knead). Cover and leave to prove for 1½ hours until doubled in size.

Heat the oven to 190°C (375°F) mark 5. Beat the dough again and then put tablespoons of it on to greased baking sheets, leaving plenty of space between each bun. Cover and leave to prove for 15 minutes. Brush with beaten egg and sprinkle with coarsely crushed cube sugar. Bake for 20 minutes. Cool on a wire rack.

CHELSEA BUNS

Makes 6

350 g (12 oz) strong plain white
    flour
75 g (3 oz) butter, melted
15 g (½ oz) fresh yeast or
    7 g (¼ oz) dried yeast
1 tsp sugar
200 ml (7 fl oz) warm milk
40 g (1½ oz) sugar
40 g (1½ oz) currants

Glaze
1 tbsp caster sugar
2 tbsp milk

Sieve the flour into a bowl and add 50 g (2 oz) of the cooled butter. Mix the fresh yeast with the sugar and add to the lukewarm milk (or sprinkle dried yeast on the milk with the sugar and leave until frothy). Add to the flour, mix well and knead thoroughly. Cover and leave for 45 minutes until the dough has doubled in size.

Heat the oven to 220°C (425°F) mark 7. Knead the dough again and shape into a rectangle about 30 x 23 cm (12 x 9 inches). Brush the surface with the remaining melted butter and sprinkle with sugar and

currants. Roll up firmly like a Swiss roll and cut across into 4-cm (1½-inch) slices. Arrange with a cut side up in a greased baking tin, close together but leaving room to swell. Cover and prove for 20 minutes. Bake for 20 minutes.

Dissolve the sugar in the milk and, while the buns are still hot, use to glaze them. Sprinkle with a little extra caster sugar and cool on a wire rack.

HOT CROSS BUNS

Makes 12

450 g (1 lb) strong plain white flour
1 tsp salt
1 tsp mixed spice
2 tsp ground cinnamon
50 g (2 oz) butter or margarine
50 g (2 oz) sugar
25 g (1 oz) fresh yeast or
    15 g (½ oz) dried yeast
175 ml (6 fl oz) warm milk
1 egg, beaten
100 g (4 oz) currants
25 g (1 oz) chopped mixed peel

Crosses
40 g (1½ oz) plain flour
3 tbsp water
1 tsp oil

Glaze
2 tbsp milk
2 tbsp caster sugar

Sieve the flour, salt, spice and cinnamon into a bowl. Rub in the fat until the mixture resembles fine breadcrumbs. Stir in the sugar, reserving 1 teaspoonful. Mix the fresh yeast with the reserved sugar and add to the lukewarm milk (or sprinkle the dried yeast on the milk with the sugar and leave until frothy). Add to the flour with the egg and mix well. Work to a soft dough, knead well. Cover and leave to prove for 1 hour.

Heat the oven to 200°C (400°F) mark 6. Work in the currants and peel, and knead well. Divide into twelve pieces. Shape into buns and place on greased baking sheets. Cover and leave to prove for 25 minutes.

To make the crosses, mix the flour, water and oil to a smooth paste. Put into a small piping bag fitted with a 5-mm (½-inch) nozzle, and pipe crosses on the risen buns. Bake for 20 minutes.

While the buns are baking, mix the milk and sugar in a pan. Simmer for 2 minutes. While the buns are hot, brush with this glaze and leave to cool on a wire rack.

SWEDISH SHROVE TUESDAY BUNS

Makes 12

350 g (12 oz) strong plain white
   flour
50 g (2 oz) sugar
25 g (1 oz) fresh yeast or
   15 g (½ oz) dried yeast
225 ml (8 fl oz) warm creamy milk
100 g (4 oz) melted butter, cooled
a little beaten egg
almond paste (see page 00)
150 ml (¼ pint) whipping cream
icing sugar for dredging

Sieve the flour into a bowl. Stir in the sugar, reserving 1 teaspoonful. Mix the fresh yeast with the sugar and add to the lukewarm milk (or sprinkle dried yeast on the milk with the sugar and leave until frothy). Add to the flour with the butter and knead until smooth and shiny. Cover and leave to prove for 1 hour.

Heat the oven to 220°C (425°F) mark 7. Knead the dough again and shape into twelve balls. Put on to greased baking sheets, cover and leave to prove for 20 minutes. Brush with a little beaten egg and bake for 15 minutes.

Cool on a wire rack and then cut a triangle from the top of each bun. Shape the almond paste into a cylinder and cut into twelve slices. Put a slice of almond paste into each triangle on top of the buns. Whip the cream to soft peaks and pipe around the edges of the triangles. Replace the cut-out triangles and dredge lightly with a little icing sugar.

LUCIA BUNS

Makes 12

350 g (12 oz) strong plain white
   flour
150 ml (¼ pint) warm milk
25 g (1 oz) fresh yeast or
   15 g (½ oz) dried yeast
50 g (2 oz) sugar
75 g (3 oz) butter, melted
½ tsp salt
pinch of saffron

Sieve the flour into a bowl. Mix the fresh yeast with 1 teaspoon of the sugar and add to half the lukewarm milk (or sprinkle dried yeast on the milk with the sugar and leave until frothy). Mix the remaining milk with the butter, sugar, salt and saffron. Add to the yeast and then work into the flour. Knead lightly to make a soft dough. Cover and prove for 1 hour.

Heat the oven to 220°C (425°F) mark 7. Knead again and break off pieces about 5 cm (2 inches) across. Roll with your

Decoration
½ tsp ground cardamom
100 g (4 oz) seedless raisins
a little beaten egg
50 g (2 oz) cube sugar

fingers into lengths about 30 cm (12 inches) long. Coil the ends in opposite directions to make an 'S' with a long body. Cross two of these pieces, putting a pinch of cardamom and some raisins where the pieces cross, and in the centre of each coil. Put on to greased baking sheets, cover and leave to prove for 20 minutes. Brush with a little beaten egg and sprinkle with crushed cube sugar. Bake for 20 minutes. Cool on a wire rack.

These buns are served by the daughters of the house on St. Lucia's Day which is celebrated in Sweden on December 13th and marks the beginning of the Christmas celebrations.

GREEK DOUGHNUTS

Makes 12

450 g (1 lb) plain flour
½ tsp salt
grated rind of 1 lemon
25 g (1 oz) fresh yeast or
    15 g (½ oz) dried yeast
1 tsp sugar
600 ml (1 pint) warm milk and
    water
1 egg, beaten
fat or oil for deep-frying

Syrup
225 g (8 oz) sugar
100 g (4 oz) clear honey
7 tbsp water
1 tbsp lemon juice
25 g (1 oz) chopped mixed nuts

Sieve the flour and salt into a bowl and stir in the lemon rind. Mix the fresh yeast with the sugar and add to the lukewarm milk and water (or sprinkle the dried yeast on the liquid with the sugar and leave until frothy). Add to the flour with the beaten egg and beat to a smooth batter. Cover and leave to prove for 20 minutes.
Beat thoroughly again. Heat a deep pan of oil and cook tablespoons of the batter for about 4 minutes until crisp and golden brown. Drain on absorbent kitchen paper and keep warm. While the doughnuts are cooking, prepare the syrup.
Heat the sugar, honey, water and lemon juice until the sugar has dissolved. Boil hard for 5 minutes. Pile the hot doughnuts on a warm plate, pour over the warm syrup, then sprinkle with nuts. Serve at once.

QUICK DOUGHNUTS

Makes 8 large and 8 small

225 g (8 oz) strong plain white flour
25 g (1 oz) margarine
1 egg, beaten
15 g (½ oz) fresh yeast or
  7 g (¼ oz) dried yeast
1 tsp sugar
50 ml (2 fl oz) warm milk
fat or oil for deep-frying
caster sugar for dredging

Sieve the flour into a warm bowl. Rub in the fat until the mixture resembles fine breadcrumbs and mix in the beaten egg. Mix the fresh yeast with the sugar and add to the milk (or sprinkle dried yeast on the milk with the sugar and leave until frothy). Add to the flour and beat well, then knead on a floured board for 10 minutes.

Roll out to 2.5 cm (1 inch) thick and cut into 7.5-cm (3-inch) rounds. Cut out the centres with a small cutter. Place rings and centres on a warm greased baking sheet, cover with a cloth and leave to rise for 20 minutes. Deep-fry in hot fat or oil until golden.

Sprinkle caster sugar thickly on to a piece of greaseproof paper. Drain the doughnut rings and miniature doughnuts using a slotted spoon and turn immediately on to the paper. Roll the doughnuts in the sugar until thoroughly coated. Serve soon after they are made.

WIGS

Makes 8

450 g (1 lb) strong plain white flour
1 tsp mixed spice
pinch of salt
7 g (¼ oz) caraway seeds
50 g (2 oz) sugar
15 g (½ oz) fresh yeast or
  7 g (¼ oz) dried yeast
300 ml (½ pint) warm milk
50 g (2 oz) butter, melted

Sieve the flour, spice and salt into a bowl. Stir in the caraway seeds and sugar, reserving 1 teaspoonful. Mix the fresh yeast with the reserved sugar and add to the lukewarm milk (or sprinkle dried yeast on the milk with the sugar and leave until frothy). Add the yeast liquid to the flour with the cooled butter. Knead well to make a soft dough. Cover and leave to prove for 1 hour.

Heat the oven to 220°C (425°F) mark 7. Knead the dough again and roll out to 2.5 cm (1 inch) thick on a floured board.

Cut out 15-cm (6-inch) rounds and cut each round into four. Place these triangles on a greased baking sheet, cover and leave to prove for 30 minutes. Bake for 20 minutes, then cool on a wire rack.

Wigs were ceremonial cakes, served with mulled ale or elderberry wine, in 17th-century England. They are mentioned by Samuel Pepys in his diary.

CREAM SPLITS

Makes 18

350 g (12 oz) strong plain white
   flour
½ tsp salt
40 g (1½ oz) sugar
40 g (1½ oz) butter
15 g (½ oz) fresh yeast or
   7 g (¼ oz) dried yeast
300 ml (½ pint) warm water
75 g (3 oz) raspberry or strawberry
   jam
150 ml (¼ pint) whipping cream
icing sugar

Sieve the flour and salt into a bowl. Stir in the sugar, reserving 1 teaspoonful. Rub in the butter until the mixture resembles fine breadcrumbs. Mix the fresh yeast with the reserved sugar and add to the lukewarm water (or sprinkle dried yeast on the water with the sugar and leave until frothy). Work into the flour and mix well to a firm dough. Knead well, cover and leave to prove for 45 minutes.

Heat the oven to 220°C (425°F) mark 7. Knead the dough again and divide into 18 pieces. Knead each piece and shape into round buns. Place on greased baking sheets, cover and leave to prove for 10 minutes. Bake for 15 minutes, then cool on a wire rack. Using a sharp knife, cut the top of each bun diagonally and spread the opening with jam. Whip the cream to soft peaks and fill each opening with cream. Dredge the tops with sieved icing sugar.

DANISH PASTRIES

Makes 16

225 g (8 oz) strong plain white flour
pinch of salt
25 g (1 oz) lard
15 g (½ oz) fresh yeast or
7 g (¼ oz) dried yeast
1 tsp sugar
5 tbsp water
1 egg, beaten
150 g (5 oz) butter

Egg wash
1 egg
2 tsp water
½ tsp sugar

Filling
almond paste (see page 35),
custard filling or spice
filling (see opposite)

glacé icing (see page 36)

Sieve the flour and salt into a bowl and rub in the lard. Mix the fresh yeast and sugar with the lukewarm water (or sprinkle the dried yeast on the water with the sugar and leave until frothy). Add to the flour along with the egg and mix to a soft dough. Knead very lightly until smooth. Cover and leave to stand for 10 minutes.

Cream the butter until soft. Roll out the dough into a 25-cm (10-inch) square. Spread the butter in a rectangle down the centre of the dough. Fold in the unbuttered sides so that they just overlap; seal the bottom and top. Roll into an oblong three times as long as it is wide. Fold evenly in three. Cover and leave to rest in a cool place for 10 minutes. Turn the dough and roll out again. Fold and rest 10 minutes. Repeat this process twice more, then rest the dough for 10 minutes and roll out ready to use. Heat the oven to 220°C (425°F) mark 7.

Prepare the egg wash by beating together the egg, sugar and water. Shape the dough in one of the following ways:

Crescents
Roll the dough into two 23-cm (9-inch) circles and cut each into eight sections. Put the chosen filling in the centre of each piece. Roll up towards the point and curl into a crescent. Place on lightly greased sheets and brush with egg wash.

Pinwheels
Roll out the dough to an oblong and spread with the spice filling. Sprinkle with currant or peel. Roll up like a Swiss roll and cut into 2.5-cm (1-inch) slices. Place on lightly greased baking sheets, cut side down, and brush with egg wash.

Twists
Prepare the dough with spice filling and fruit as for Pinwheels. Fold the dough into three. Cut into 16 strips parallel to the open sides. Twist each strip, place on lightly greased baking sheets, brush with egg wash.

Envelopes
Cut the dough into 7.5-cm (3-inch) squares. Put the chosen filling in the centre of each square. Fold four corners to the centre and press down well. Place on lightly greased baking sheets and brush with egg wash.

Cover the pastries and leave to prove for 20 minutes, then bake for 15 minutes until golden brown. Ice with glacé icing (see page 36) or brush with a little apricot jam while still hot. Leave to cool.

CUSTARD FILLING (for Danish Pastries)

1 egg yolk
1 tbsp sugar
1 tbsp plain flour
150 ml (¼ pint) milk
a few drops of vanilla essence

Blend together the egg yolk, sugar, flour and milk. Cook over a low heat until thick and creamy and flavour with a few drops of vanilla essence. Use as required in the recipe above.

SPICE FILLING (for Danish Pastries)

25 g (1 oz) butter
25 g (1 oz) icing sugar
1 tsp ground cinnamon

Cream together the butter, icing sugar and cinnamon. Use as required in the recipe opposite.

CHOCOLATE CROISSANTS

Makes 8

*300 g (10 oz) strong plain white
  flour*
pinch of salt
*15 g (½ oz) fresh yeast or
  7 g (¼ oz) dried yeast*
1 tsp sugar
225 ml (8 fl oz) warm milk
150 g (5 oz) butter
*100 g (4 oz) plain chocolate,
  chopped*
a little beaten egg to glaze

Sieve the flour and salt into a bowl. Mix the fresh yeast and sugar and add to the lukewarm milk (or sprinkle dried yeast on the milk with the sugar and leave until frothy). Melt 25 g (1 oz) of the butter, and add to the flour; mix to a soft dough. Knead lightly, cover and leave to prove for 30 minutes.

Knead the dough again and roll into a rectangle. Divide the remaining butter into three portions. Dot one portion over the top two-thirds of the dough. Fold up the bottom third of the dough and then the top third down on this. Press the edges together, and give a quarter-turn to the dough. Roll out again and repeat the process twice more. Between each rolling, cover the dough and leave in a cool place for 10 minutes.

Heat the oven to 230°C (450°F) mark 8. Roll the dough out thinly and cut into triangles with 15-cm (6-inch) bases and 23-cm (9-inch) sides. Place a few pieces of chocolate at the base of each triangle and roll up from the base. Curl the ends to form a crescent. Place on lightly greased baking sheets, cover and leave to prove for 20 minutes. Brush with beaten egg and bake for 15 minutes. Cool on a wire rack and eat freshly baked.

ORANGE TWISTS

Makes 40

450 g (1 lb) strong plain white flour
½ tsp salt
25 g (1 oz) fresh yeast or
    15 g (½ oz) dried yeast
1 tsp sugar
225 ml (8 fl oz) warm milk
225 g (8 oz) butter
1 egg
1 egg yolk

Filling
175 g (6 oz) ground almonds
grated rind and juice of 1 orange
2 tbsp orange liqueur
25 g (1 oz) chopped candied orange
    peel
1 egg white

Glaze
40 g (1½ oz) icing sugar
1 tbsp orange juice
50 g (2 oz) toasted flaked almonds

Sieve the flour and salt into a bowl. Mix the fresh yeast with the sugar and add to the lukewarm milk (or sprinkle the dried yeast on the milk with the sugar and leave until frothy). Melt 50 g (2 oz) of the butter and add to the flour with the egg and knead to a smooth dough. Cover and leave to prove for 15 minutes.

Knead again and roll out to a rectangle 35 x 20 cm (14 x 8 inches). Dot half the remaining butter over the top two-thirds of this rectangle. Fold up the bottom third, and turn the top third down on this. Press the edges, give a quarter-turn to the dough and roll out to a rectangle again. Repeat the process once more with the remaining butter, and then again without any butter. Fold in three again, then roll out to a rectangle 50 x 40 cm (20 x 16 inches). Heat the oven to 220°C (425°F) mark 7.

Mix the ground almonds, orange rind and juice, liqueur, peel and egg white. Cut the dough into four 50-cm (20-inch) strips, then each strip into five pieces, giving twenty 10-cm (4-inch) squares. Cut each square across to make two triangles.

Place a little almond filling in the centre of each one and roll up from the long side. Place on greased baking sheets, curving slightly to give a crescent shape. Cover and leave to prove for 15 minutes. Brush with beaten egg yolk and bake for 15 minutes. While still warm, glaze with the icing sugar mixed with orange juice, and sprinkle with almonds. Leave to cool.

FRUIT BREADS AND YEAST CAKES

Sweet breads with dried fruit or other flavourings have been popular for centuries. The earliest fruit breads were simply made by wrapping dough around fat, sugar and dried fruit, or by kneading these into the dough. Caraway seeds, saffron and nuts were also popular flavourings. In Europe, a lighter sponge-type cake was made with yeast to serve as a party dish.

CURRANT BREAD

Makes two 450-g (1-lb) loaves

450 g (1 lb) strong plain white flour
1 tsp salt
25 g (1 oz) sugar
25 g (1 oz) butter
25 g (1 oz) fresh yeast or
    15 g (½ oz) dried yeast
300 ml (½ pint) warm milk and
    water
100 g (4 oz) currants
a little clear honey to glaze

Sieve the flour and salt into a bowl and stir in the sugar, reserving 1 teaspoonful. Rub in the butter until the mixture resembles fine breadcrumbs. Mix the fresh yeast with the reserved sugar and add to the lukewarm milk and water (or sprinkle dried yeast on the liquid with the sugar and leave until frothy). Add to the flour with the currants and work to a firm dough. Knead until smooth, cover and leave to prove for 45 minutes.

Heat the oven to 220°C (425°F) mark 7. Knead the dough again and divide into two pieces. Shape each piece to fit a greased 450-g (1-lb) loaf tin. Cover and leave to prove for 30 minutes. Bake for 40 minutes. While the loaves are hot, brush the tops with a wet brush dipped into a little clear honey. Cool on a wire rack.

ORANGE BREAD

Makes one 900-g (2-lb) loaf

450 g (1 lb) strong plain white flour
½ tsp salt
25 g (1 oz) sugar
15 g (½ oz) fresh yeast or
    7 g (¼ oz) dried yeast
150 ml (¼ pint) warm water
grated rind and juice of 1 large
    orange
1 egg, beaten
175 g (6 oz) sultanas
a little clear honey to glaze

Sieve the flour and salt into a bowl. Stir in the sugar, reserving 1 teaspoonful. Mix the fresh yeast with the reserved sugar and add to the lukewarm water (or sprinkle dried yeast on the water with the sugar and leave until frothy). Add to the flour with the orange rind and juice, the egg and sultanas. Mix thoroughly and knead well. Cover and leave to prove for 1 hour.

Heat the oven to 200°C (400°F) mark 6. Knead the dough again and shape to fit a greased 900-g (2-lb) loaf tin. Cover and prove for 30 minutes. Bake for 40 minutes. While the loaf is hot, brush the top with a wet brush dipped in a little clear honey. Cool on a wire rack.

GRANNY LOAF

Makes two 900-g (2-lb) loaves

800 g (1 lb 12 oz) strong plain
  white flour
1 tsp ground cinnamon
1 tsp ground mace
1 tsp ground ginger
½ tsp ground nutmeg
225 g (8 oz) dark soft brown sugar
100 g (4 oz) butter
100 g (4 oz) lard
25 g (1 oz) fresh yeast or
  15 g (½ oz) dried yeast
450 ml (¾ pint) warm milk and
  water
1 egg, beaten
350 g (12 oz) currants
175 g (6 oz) stoned raisins
175 g (6 oz) sultanas
50 g (2 oz) chopped mixed peel

Sieve the flour and spices into a bowl then stir in the sugar, reserving 1 teaspoonful. Rub in the butter and lard until the mixture resembles fine breadcrumbs. Mix the fresh yeast with the reserved sugar and add to the lukewarm milk and water (or sprinkle dried yeast on the milk with the sugar and leave until frothy). Add to the flour with the egg and work to a soft dough. Knead well, cover and leave to prove for 1 hour.

Heat the oven to 220°C (425°F) mark 7. Work the dried fruit and peel into the dough and knead well. Divide the dough in half and shape to fit two greased 900-g (2-lb) loaf tins. Cover and leave to prove for 45 minutes. Bake for 20 minutes, then reduce the temperature to 190°C (375°F) mark 5 and continue baking for 1 hour. Cool on a wire rack.

It is worth making two large loaves, as suggested here. They keep fresh for weeks, and are delicious plain or toasted and buttered, or served with cheese.

COCONUT BREAD

Makes one 900-g (2-lb) loaf

450 g (1 lb) strong plain white flour
½ tsp salt
75 g (3 oz) desiccated coconut
25 g (1 oz) sugar
15 g (½ oz) fresh yeast or
  7 g (¼ oz) dried yeast
300 ml (½ pint) warm milk and
  water
a little clear honey to glaze

Sieve the flour and salt into a bowl and stir in the coconut, reserving 2 teaspoonfuls. Stir in the sugar, but reserve 1 teaspoonful. Mix the fresh yeast with the reserved sugar and add to the lukewarm milk and water (or sprinkle dried yeast on the liquid with the sugar and leave until frothy). Work into the flour mixture to form a dough and knead well. Cover and leave to prove for 1 hour.

Heat the oven to 200°C (400°F) mark 6. Knead the dough again and shape to fit a greased 900-g (2-lb) loaf tin. Cover and leave to prove for 30 minutes. Bake for 40 minutes. While the loaf is hot, brush the top with a wet brush dipped in a little clear honey and sprinkle with the reserved coconut. Cool on a wire rack.

SCANDINAVIAN YULE BREAD

Makes 3 loaves

50 g (12 oz) strong plain white
  flour
 tsp salt
00 g (1 lb 12 oz) rye flour
0 g (2 oz) butter
75 ml (1½ pints) stout
25 g (8 oz) black treacle
rated rind of 2 oranges
 tbsp ground aniseed
5 g (3 oz) fresh yeast or
  40 g (1½ oz) dried yeast
 tsp sugar
 tbsp warm water

Glaze
 tbsp black treacle
 tbsp warm water

Sieve the white flour into a bowl with the salt; mix in the rye flour. Remove 100 g (4 oz) of the flour to a smaller bowl. Put the butter, stout and treacle into a pan and heat until it is lukewarm and the fat has melted. Add to the larger quantity of flour with the orange rind and aniseed. Mix the fresh yeast with the sugar and add to the lukewarm water (or sprinkle dried yeast on the water with the sugar and leave until frothy). Mix into the flour, and work to a firm dough. Cover and prove for 1½ hours.

Knead the dough with the reserved flour until it is smooth and glossy. Divide the mixture into three pieces and shape into long loaves. Put on greased baking sheets, cover and leave to prove for 1 hour. Prick the surfaces with a skewer. Heat the oven to 160°C (325°F) mark 3. Bake the loaves for 30 minutes, then brush the surface of the loaves with the black treacle dissolved in water. Return to the oven and cook for a further 30 minutes. Glaze when the loaves are baked. Wrap the loaves in clean towels and cool on wire racks. This helps keep the loaves soft.

VICTORIAN DOUGH CAKE

Makes one 900-g (2-lb) cake

450 g (1 lb) risen white bread dough
  (see page 15)
1 tsp mixed spice
50 g (2 oz) butter, softened
50 g (2 oz) caster sugar
100 g (4 oz) mixed dried fruit
a little clear honey to glaze

Work the spice, butter, sugar and dried fruit into the dough until evenly mixed. Shape to fit a greased 900-g (2-lb) loaf tin. Cover and leave to prove for 30 minutes.

Heat the oven to 200°C (400°F) mark 6. Bake for 40 minutes. Remove from the oven. While the loaf is hot, brush the top with a wet brush dipped into a little clear honey. Cool on a wire rack.

CHOCOLATE HORSESHOE RING

Makes 1

225 g (8 oz) strong plain white flour
pinch of salt
40 g (1½ oz) butter
15 g (½ oz) fresh yeast or
  7 g (¼ oz) dried yeast
1 tsp sugar
4 tbsp warm milk
1 egg, beaten
100 g (4 oz) plain chocolate
50 g (2 oz) flaked almonds
50 g (2 oz) seedless raisins
175 g (6 oz) icing sugar
grated chocolate to decorate

Sieve the flour and salt into a bowl. Rub in 25 g (1 oz) of the butter until the mixture resembles fine breadcrumbs. Mix the fresh yeast with the sugar and add to the lukewarm milk (or sprinkle dried yeast on the milk with the sugar and leave until frothy). Add to the flour with the egg and mix well. Knead until smooth, cover and leave to prove for 45 minutes.

Heat the oven to 220°C (425°F) mark 7. Chop two-thirds of the chocolate finely and grate the rest. Mix the chopped chocolate with the almonds and raisins. Knead the dough again and roll out into a rectangle 40 x 20 cm (16 x 8 inches). Melt the remaining butter and use to brush over the dough. Sprinkle with the filling and roll up firmly, starting with one long side. Seal the edges by pinching firmly. Lift on to a greased baking sheet and form into a horseshoe, with the join underneath. Cover and leave to prove for 30 minutes. Bake for 30 minutes. Cool on a wire rack. Melt the icing sugar with a little water and spread on top, then sprinkle with grated chocolate. Leave to set.

GUGELHUPF

Makes 1 cake

225 g (8 oz) strong plain white flour
25 g (1 oz) fresh yeast or
  15 g (½ oz) dried yeast
1 tsp sugar
6 tbsp warm milk
50 g (2 oz) seedless raisins
1 tbsp rum
50 g (2 oz) butter, melted
50 g (2 oz) sugar
2 eggs
grated rind and juice of 1 orange
fine breadcrumbs or semolina
icing sugar to dredge

Sieve the flour into a bowl, then remove 50 g (2 oz) of the flour to a smaller bowl. Mix the fresh yeast with 1 teaspoon sugar and add to the lukewarm milk (or sprinkle dried yeast on the milk with the sugar and leave until frothy). Mix the yeast liquid with the flour in the small bowl, cover and leave to rise for 30 minutes.

Meanwhile, soak the raisins in the rum. Beat the butter, sugar, eggs, orange rind and juice into the yeast mixture, and then add the soaked raisins and remaining flour. Beat well to form a soft dough. Place in a greased ring mould which has been lightly coated with breadcrumbs or semolina. Heat the oven to 200°C (400°F) mark 6. Cover the dough and leave to prove for 30 minutes.

Bake for 40 minutes. Turn out carefully, cool on a wire rack and dredge thickly with icing sugar.

This cake is traditionally made in a tall, fluted ring tin, but a plain ring tin may be used. Sometimes a pattern of almonds is arranged in the base of the tin before the cake mixture is put in.

FRUIT KUCHEN

Makes 2 cakes

225 g (8 oz) strong plain white flour
pinch of salt
25 g (1 oz) fresh yeast or
   15 g (½ oz) dried yeast
25 g (1 oz) sugar
6 tbsp warm milk
25 g (1 oz) butter, melted
1 egg
grated rind of 1 lemon

Topping
25 g (1 oz) caster sugar
450 g (1 lb) eating apples, or 225 g
   (½ lb) each plums and apricots
1 tbsp ground cinnamon

Sieve the flour and salt into a bowl. Mix the fresh yeast with 1 teaspoon of the sugar and add to the lukewarm milk (or sprinkle dried yeast on the milk with the sugar and leave until frothy). Add to the flour with the remaining sugar, butter, egg and lemon rind. Knead to a soft dough. Cover and leave to prove for 1½ hours.

Heat the oven to 200°C (400°F) mark 6. Knead the dough again and shape to fit two greased 18-cm (7-inch) sandwich tins. Sprinkle with a little of the sugar and then cover with slices of peeled apple, or halved and stoned plums and apricots arranged close together. Sprinkle with a mixture of the remaining sugar and the cinnamon. Bake for 20 minutes, then reduce the temperature to 190°C (375°F) mark 5 and continue baking for 20 minutes. Serve while still slightly warm and freshly baked.

PANETTONE

Makes 1 cake

350 g (12 oz) strong plain white
   flour
pinch of salt
50 g (2 oz) sugar
25 g (1 oz) fresh yeast or
   7 g (½ oz) dried yeast
150 ml (¼ pint) warm milk
50 g (2 oz) butter, melted
3 egg yolks
75 g (3 oz) seedless raisins
50 g (2 oz) chopped mixed peel
grated rind of 1 lemon
a little beaten egg to glaze

Sieve the flour and salt into a bowl and stir in the sugar, reserving 1 teaspoonful. Mix the fresh yeast with the reserved sugar and lukewarm milk (or sprinkle dried yeast on the milk with the sugar and leave until frothy). Add to the flour with the melted butter, egg yolks, raisins, peel and lemon rind. Mix well to form a stiff dough. Knead well, cover and leave to prove for 2 hours.

Heat the oven to 220°C (425°F) mark 7. Shape the dough into a tall domed loaf and place on a greased baking sheet. Glaze the bread well with beaten egg. Bake for 15 minutes, then reduce the temperature to 190°C (375°F) mark 5 and continue baking for 25 minutes. Cool on a wire rack.

This Italian speciality is a delicious cake-bread which is served on festive occasions such as Easter and Christmas. It is sold in characteristically tall blue boxes, and keeps very well. It is also delicious when toasted.

MARZIPAN WHIRL

Makes 1

350 g (12 oz) strong plain white
    flour
pinch of salt
grated rind of ½ lemon
50 g (2 oz) caster sugar
50 g (2 oz) butter, melted
25 g (1 oz) fresh yeast or
    15 g (½ oz) dried yeast
5 tbsp warm milk

Filling
225 g (8 oz) ground almonds
2 egg whites
50 g (2 oz) caster sugar
2 tbsp rum

Glaze
40 g (1½ oz) icing sugar
1 tbsp lemon juice
2 tbsp water

Sieve the flour and salt into a bowl. Stir in the lemon rind and sugar, reserving 1 teaspoonful. Mix the fresh yeast with the reserved sugar and add to the lukewarm milk (or sprinkle the dried yeast on the milk with the sugar and leave until frothy). Add to the flour with the melted butter. Mix to a dough and knead lightly. Cover and leave to prove for 45 minutes.

Heat the oven to 200°C (400°F) mark 6. Knead the dough again and roll out to a rectangle 45 x 30 cm (18 x 12 inches). Mix the almonds, egg whites, caster sugar and rum together. Spread this mixture over the dough and roll up firmly, lengthways. Cut in half, and twist the lengths together like a rope. Put on a greased baking sheet, cover and leave to prove for 20 minutes. Bake for 35 minutes. While still warm, glaze the top with a mixture of icing sugar, lemon juice and water. Cool on a wire rack.

CINNAMON RING

Makes 1

225 g (8 oz) strong plain white flour
pinch of salt
75 g (3 oz) sugar
4 tbsp warm milk
15 g (½ oz) fresh yeast or
   7 g (¼ oz) dried yeast
25 g (1 oz) butter, melted
1 egg, beaten

Filling
25 g (1 oz) butter, melted
25 g (1 oz) sugar
1 tsp ground cinnamon
a little beaten egg to glaze

Sieve the flour and salt into a bowl and stir in the sugar, reserving 1 teaspoonful. Mix the fresh yeast with the reserved sugar and add to the lukewarm milk (or sprinkle dried yeast on the milk with the sugar and leave until frothy). Add to the flour with the melted butter and egg and work to a soft dough. Cover and prove for 1 hour.

Heat the oven to 200°C (400°F) mark 6. Knead the dough again and roll out to a thin rectangle. Brush with melted butter and sprinkle with the sugar and cinnamon. Roll up like a Swiss roll and form into a ring, joining the ends firmly. Put on a greased baking sheet and snip the top with scissors at 2.5-cm (1-inch) intervals. Pull the snipped pieces to alternate sides. Cover and leave to prove for 45 minutes. Brush with beaten egg. Bake for 25 minutes. Cool on a wire rack.

MALT BREAD

Makes two 450-g (1-lb) loaves

450 g (1 lb) strong plain white flour
1 tsp salt
25 g (1 oz) fresh yeast or
   15 g (½ oz) dried yeast
1 tsp sugar
175 ml (6 fl oz) warm water
75 g (3 oz) malt extract
2 tbsp black treacle
25 g (1 oz) butter
225 g (8 oz) sultanas
a little clear honey

Sieve the flour and salt into a bowl. Mix the fresh yeast with the sugar and add to the lukewarm water (or sprinkle dried yeast on the water with the sugar and leave until frothy). Warm together the malt extract, treacle and butter until the fat has melted, and leave until lukewarm. Add to the flour with the yeast liquid and work to a soft dough. If it is very sticky, add a little more flour, but be sure that the dough remains soft and spongy. Cover and leave to prove for 45 minutes.

Heat the oven to 200°C (400°F) mark 6. Knead the sultanas into the dough and divide into two pieces. Knead each piece and shape to fit two greased 450-g (1-lb) tins. Cover and leave to prove for 45 minutes. Bake for 45 minutes. While the loaves are hot, brush the tops with a wet brush dipped into a little clear honey. Cool on a wire rack.

SAFFRON ALMOND BREAD

Makes 1 loaf

150 ml (¼ pint) milk
25 g (1 oz) fresh yeast or
   15 g (½ oz) dried yeast
1 tsp sugar
225 g (8 oz) strong plain white flour
pinch of saffron
25 g (1 oz) butter, melted
50 g (2 oz) sugar
1 egg, beaten
25 g (1 oz) seedless raisins
25 g (1 oz) ground almonds

Topping
1 egg, beaten
50 g (2 oz) chopped blanched
   almonds
25 g (1 oz) sugar, granulated or
   caster

Heat half the milk to lukewarm and add the fresh yeast mixed with 1 teaspoon sugar, (or sprinkle dried yeast on the milk with the sugar and leave until frothy). Add just enough of the flour to make a smooth paste. Cover and leave in a warm place for 30 minutes. Warm the remaining milk and add the crushed saffron. Sieve the remaining flour into a bowl. Add the cooled butter to the flour with the saffron milk, sugar, egg, raisins and almonds. Add the yeast mixture and knead to a soft dough. Cover and leave to prove for 1½ hours.

Heat the oven to 200°C (400°F) mark 6. Knead the dough again and divide into three pieces. Roll each piece into a 'sausage' shape and plait together. Put on a greased baking sheet, cover and prove for 30 minutes. Brush the plait thickly with beaten egg and sprinkle with almonds and sugar (granulated will give a coarser topping than caster). Bake for 30 minutes. Cool on a wire rack.

LINCOLNSHIRE CHRISTMAS LOAF

Makes one 900-g (2-lb) loaf

450 g (1 lb) strong plain white flour
pinch of salt
25 g (1 oz) fresh yeast or
  15 g (½ oz) dried yeast
225 g (8 oz) butter, diced
225 g (8 oz) sugar
225 g (8 oz) currants
25 g (1 oz) chopped mixed peel
1 egg
1 tsp bicarbonate of soda
150 ml (¼ pint) warm milk

Heat the oven to 180°C (350°F) mark 4. Sieve together the flour and salt. Rub in the fresh yeast, or stir in the dried yeast. Rub the butter into the flour until the mixture resembles fine breadcrumbs. Stir in the sugar, currants and peel. Beat the egg and work into the mixture. Dissolve the soda in the lukewarm milk and work into the cake mixture. Put into a greased and lined 900-g (2-lb) loaf tin. Bake for 1½ hours. Cool on a wire rack.

GERMAN PARTY CAKE

Makes 1

350 g (12 oz) strong plain white
  flour
100 g (4 oz) caster sugar
175 g (6 oz) butter, melted
pinch of salt
grated rind of ½ lemon
175 g (6 oz) currants
15 g (½ oz) fresh yeast or
  7 g (¼ oz) dried yeast
5 tbsp warm milk
3 eggs, beaten

Topping
175 g (6 oz) plain chocolate
25 g (1 oz) flaked almonds

Sieve the flour into a bowl then stir in the sugar, reserving 1 teaspoonful. Add the melted butter, salt, lemon rind and currants. Mix the fresh yeast with the reserved sugar and add to the lukewarm milk (or sprinkle the dried yeast on the milk with the sugar and leave until frothy). Add to the flour with the eggs and beat well until the mixture bubbles. Cover and leave to prove for 40 minutes.

Heat the oven to 180°C (350°F) mark 4. Put the dough into a greased 23-cm (9-inch) ring mould or gugelhupf tin. Bake for 1 hour. Cool on a wire rack.

Melt the chocolate in a bowl over hot water or in a microwave, and pour over the cake so that it is completely covered. Sprinkle with the almonds and leave to set.

RUM BABAS

Makes 12

225 g (8 oz) strong plain white flour
½ tsp salt
25 g (1 oz) fresh yeast or
    15 g (½ oz) dried yeast
25 g (1 oz) caster sugar
6 tbsp warm milk
100 g (4 oz) butter, softened
4 eggs, beaten
100 g (4 oz) currants

Finishing
450 g (1 lb) sugar
450 g (¾ pint) water
4 tbsp rum
75 g (3 oz) apricot jam
1 tbsp water
150 ml (¼ pint) whipping cream
glacé cherries

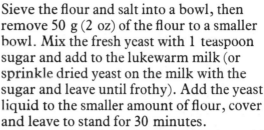

Sieve the flour and salt into a bowl, then remove 50 g (2 oz) of the flour to a smaller bowl. Mix the fresh yeast with 1 teaspoon sugar and add to the lukewarm milk (or sprinkle dried yeast on the milk with the sugar and leave until frothy). Add the yeast liquid to the smaller amount of flour, cover and leave to stand for 30 minutes.

Grease 12 dariole (castle pudding) moulds and half-fill them with dough. Cover and leave to prove for 40 minutes.

Heat the oven to 200°C (400°F) mark 6. Bake for 15 minutes or until the babas begin to shrink from the sides of the moulds then leave to cool in the tins for 5 minutes. Trim tops evenly and turn out on to a plate and leave to cool.

While the babas are cooking, prepare the rum syrup by dissolving the sugar in the water over a low heat. Bring to the boil and boil for 1 minute. Remove from the heat and stir in the rum. Leave until lukewarm.

Prick the babas all over with a finely pointed skewer and pour over the warm rum syrup. Turn the babas carefully to ensure they are well soaked. Leave to cool.

Warm the apricot jam and water together and rub through a sieve. Brush the surfaces of the cooled babas with warm glaze. Whip the cream, pipe a whirl on top of each baba, and decorate the whirl with a cherry.

Sometimes babas are baked in individual ring moulds. Babas keep well. You can store them, prior to being soaked in syrup, for up to two weeks in an airtight container; or they can be frozen. Once the babas have been soaked in syrup, they can be kept, tightly covered, for up to 24 hours.

SAVARIN

Makes 1 cake

225 g (8 oz) strong plain white flour
½ tsp salt
25 g (1 oz) fresh yeast or
  15 g (½ oz) dried yeast
25 g (1 oz) caster sugar
6 tbsp warm milk
100 g (4 oz) butter, softened
4 eggs, beaten

Finishing
450 g (1 lb) sugar
450 ml (¾ pint) water
150 ml (¼ pint) rum
75 g (3 oz) apricot jam
1 tbsp water
225 g (8 oz) hulled strawberries
100 g (4 oz) grapes
3 slices fresh pineapple
whipped cream

Sieve the flour and salt into a bowl. Remove 50 g (2 oz) of the flour to a smaller bowl. Mix the fresh yeast with 1 teaspoon of the sugar and add to the lukewarm milk (or sprinkle dried yeast on the milk with the sugar and leave until frothy). Add the yeast liquid to the smaller amount of flour, cover and leave to stand for 30 minutes.

Heat the oven to 200°C (400°F) mark 6. Add the flour, remaining sugar, butter and eggs to the yeast batter and beat thoroughly for 5 minutes. Grease a 23-cm (9-inch) ring mould and hall-fill with the dough. Cover and leave to prove for 40 minutes. Bake for 25 minutes. Leave to cool in the tin for 5 minutes, then turn on to a wire rack to cool.

While the savarin is cooking, prepare the rum syrup by dissolving the sugar in the water over a low heat. Bring to the boil and boil hard for 1 minute. Remove from the heat and stir in the rum. Use while hot.

Prick all over the savarin with a finely pointed skewer. Stand the wire rack over a large plate, and pour the hot syrup over the savarin. Keep pouring on any syrup which runs into the plate, but reserve the last 150 ml (¼ pint).

Warm the apricot jam and water together and rub through a sieve. Brush the surface of the savarin with the glaze. Halve the strawberries, halve and de-pip the grapes, and cut the pineapple into small chunks. Mix the fruit with the reserved syrup and pile into the centre of the savarin. Serve with whipped cream.

YULE BREAD

Makes one 900-g (2-lb) loaf

350 g (12 oz) strong plain white
*   flour*
pinch of salt
100 g (4 oz) butter
100 g (4 oz) sugar
15 g (½ oz) fresh yeast or
*   7 g (¼ oz) dried yeast*
150 ml (¼ pint) warm milk
1 egg, beaten
175 g (6 oz) currants
100 g (4 oz) sultanas
50 g (2 oz) chopped mixed peel
½ tsp ground cinnamon
¼ tsp ground nutmeg

Sieve the flour and salt into a bowl. Rub in the butter until the mixture resembles fine breadcrumbs then stir in the sugar, reserving 1 teaspoonful. Mix the fresh yeast with the reserved sugar and add to the lukewarm milk (or sprinkle dried yeast on the milk with the sugar and leave until frothy). Add to the flour with the beaten egg and work to a soft dough. Cover and leave to prove for 1 hour.

Heat the oven to 220°C (425°F) mark 7. Work the currants, sultanas, peel and spices into the dough and knead well. Shape to fit a greased 900-g (2-lb) loaf tin. Cover and leave to prove for 45 minutes. Bake for 20 minutes, then reduce the temperature to 190°C (375°F) mark 5 and continue baking for 1 hour. Cool on a wire rack.

This loaf was the forerunner of today's Christmas cake, and was much enjoyed in farmhouses with mulled ale or wine and wedges of cheese.

BARM BRACK

Makes one 900-g (2-lb) cake

450 g (1 lb) risen white bread dough
*   (see page 15)*
75 g (3 oz) sugar
75 g (3 oz) lard
3 eggs, beaten
50 g (2 oz) stoned raisins
50 g (2 oz) chopped mixed peel

Work the sugar and lard into the dough. Add the beaten eggs, a little at a time, and then the raisins and peel. Work together until well mixed. Shape to fit a greased 900-g (2-lb) loaf tin. Cover and leave to prove for 45 minutes.

Heat the oven to 220°C (425°F) mark 7. Bake for 30 minutes, then reduce the temperature to 180°C (350°F) mark 4 and continue baking for 30 minutes. Cool on a wire rack.

STOLLEN

Makes 1

225 g (8 oz) strong plain white flour
¼ tsp salt
25 g (1 oz) butter or margarine
grated rind of 1 lemon
15 g (½ oz) fresh yeast or
*   7 g (¼ oz) dried yeast*
1 tsp sugar
150 ml (¼ pint) warm milk
1 egg, beaten
50 g (2 oz) currants
50 g (2 oz) sultanas
25 g (1 oz) chopped mixed peel
25 g (1 oz) blanched almonds,
*   chopped*
icing sugar to dredge

Reserve 50 g (2 oz) of the flour and sieve the rest with the salt into a bowl. Rub in the fat and stir in the lemon rind. Mix the fresh yeast with the sugar and lukewarm milk (or sprinkle the dried yeast on the milk with the sugar and leave until frothy). Add the reserved flour, cover and leave to stand for 30 minutes. Add to the fat and flour mixture with the beaten egg, currants, sultanas, peel and almonds. Knead until smooth, cover and leave to prove for 1 hour.

Heat the oven to 200°C (400°F) mark 6. Knead the dough again until smooth. Roll out to an oval 23 x 18 cm (9 x 7 inches) and fold in half lengthways. Place on a greased baking sheet, cover and leave to prove for 40 minutes. Bake for 30 minutes. Cool on a wire rack. Dredge very thickly with sieved icing sugar.

WALNUT DOUGH CAKE

Makes two 450-g (1-lb) cakes

225 g (8 oz) wholemeal flour
175 g (6 oz) strong plain white flour
½ tsp salt
75 g (3 oz) lard
100 g (4 oz) light soft brown sugar
75 g (3 oz) chopped walnuts
75 g (3 oz) stoned raisins
25 g (1 oz) fresh yeast or
*   15 g (½ oz) dried yeast*
300 ml (½ pint) warm milk
1 egg, beaten

Mix the flours and salt together in a bowl then rub in the lard until the mixture resembles fine breadcrumbs. Stir in the sugar, reserving 1 teaspoonful and then add the walnuts and raisins. Mix the fresh yeast with the reserved sugar and add to the lukewarm water (or sprinkle dried yeast on the milk with the sugar and leave until frothy). Add to the flour mixture with the egg, and mix thoroughly. Cover and leave to prove for 30 minutes.

Heat the oven to 220°C (425°F) mark 7. Beat the dough with a wooden spoon (or use a mixer dough hook) until smooth and elastic. Divide the mixture between two greased 450-g (1-lb) loaf tins, cover and leave to prove for 45 minutes. Bake for 15 minutes, then reduce the temperature to 190°C (375°F) mark 5 and continue baking for 45 minutes. Cool on a wire rack.

FAMILY YEAST CAKE

Makes 1

350 g (12 oz) strong plain white
  flour
½ tsp salt
50 g (2 oz) caster sugar
75 g (3 oz) butter or margarine
175 g (6 oz) mixed dried fruit
grated rind of 1 orange
2 eggs, beaten
25 g (1 oz) fresh yeast or
  15 g (½ oz) dried yeast
6 tbsp milk

Topping
2 tbsp jam
25 g (1 oz) butter
25 g (1 oz) sugar
40 g (1½ oz) plain flour
1 tsp ground cinnamon

Sieve the flour and salt into a bowl then stir in the sugar, reserving 1 teaspoonful. Rub in the butter until the mixture resembles fine breadcrumbs. Stir in the dried fruit, orange rind and eggs. Mix the fresh yeast with reserved sugar and add to the lukewarm milk (or sprinkle dried yeast on the milk with the sugar and leave until frothy). Mix into the flour to give a very soft dough. Put into a greased 20-cm (8-inch) square tin lined with greased greaseproof paper. Cover and leave to prove for 1½ hours.

Heat the oven to 200°C (400°F) mark 6. Spread the top of the cake lightly with jam. For the topping: cream the butter and sugar, and work in the flour and cinnamon to make a crumble mixture. Sprinkle on top of the dough and bake for 45 minutes. Cool in the tin for 10 minutes, then turn out the cake carefully and continue cooling on a wire rack.

STREUSEL

Makes 1 large or 2 small cakes

225 g (8 oz) strong plain white flour
1 tsp salt
25 g (1 oz) fresh yeast or
    15 g (½ oz) dried yeast
25 g (1 oz) sugar
6 tbsp warm milk
100 g (4 oz) butter, softened
2 eggs, beaten
grated rind of 1 lemon

Topping
25 g (1 oz) butter, melted
25 g (1 oz) plain flour
175 g (6 oz) caster sugar
1 tbsp ground cinnamon

Sieve the flour and salt into a bowl. Mix the fresh yeast with 1 teaspoon of the sugar and add to the lukewarm milk (or sprinkle dried yeast on the milk with the sugar and leave until frothy). Add to the flour with the remaining sugar, butter, eggs and lemon rind and mix to form a soft dough. Knead well, cover and leave to prove for 1½ hours.

Heat the oven to 200°C (400°F) mark 6. Knead the dough again and shape to fit a greased rectangular tin 30 x 23 cm (12 x 9 inches) or two 18-cm (7-inch) sandwich tins. Cover and leave to prove for 30 minutes.

Brush the surface with melted butter. Mix any remaining butter with the flour, sugar and cinnamon to make a crumble mixture. Sprinkle thickly over the cake. Bake for 30 minutes. Serve while still slightly warm and freshly baked.

ICED TWIST

Makes 1

225 g (8 oz) strong plain white flour
pinch of salt
15 g (½ oz) fresh yeast or
    7 g (¼ oz) dried yeast
1 tsp sugar
100 ml (4 fl oz) warm milk
25 g (1 oz) butter, melted
1 egg, beaten
50 g (2 oz) sugar
a little milk to glaze
175 g (6 oz) icing sugar
glacé cherries, angelica and nuts

Sieve the flour and salt into a bowl. Mix the fresh yeast with the sugar and add to the lukewarm milk (or sprinkle dried yeast on the milk with the sugar and leave until frothy). Add to the flour with the cooled butter, egg and sugar, and mix well. Knead thoroughly, cover and leave to prove for 45 minutes.

Heat the oven to 220°C (425°F) mark 7. Knead the dough again and divide into three even-sized pieces. With the hands, shape each piece into a 'sausage'. Plait the pieces of dough, tucking the ends under firmly. Place on a greased baking sheet, cover and leave to prove for 15 minutes.

Brush with milk and bake for 20 minutes. Cool on a wire rack.

Ice with the sieved icing sugar mixed with a little water or lemon juice, and decorate with cherries, angelica and nuts. Leave to set.

WHOLEMEAL GINGER LOAF

Makes two 450-g (1-lb) loaves

350 g (12 oz) wholemeal flour
100 g (4 oz) strong plain white flour
1 tsp salt
25 g (1 oz) butter
50 g (2 oz) black treacle
75 g (3 oz) sultanas
2 tsp ground ginger
15 g (½ oz) fresh yeast or
   7 g (¼ oz) dried yeast
1 tsp sugar
300 ml (½ pint) warm water

Topping
25 g (1 oz) butter
25 g (1 oz) demerara sugar
40 g (1½ oz) plain flour

Mix the flours and salt together in a bowl. Warm the butter and treacle together until just runny and work into the mixture with the sultanas and ginger. Mix the fresh yeast with the sugar and add to the lukewarm water (or sprinkle the dried yeast on the water with the sugar and leave until frothy). Add to the flour and mix to a soft dough. Knead well, cover and leave to prove for 1 hour.

Heat the oven to 200°C (400°F) mark 6. Divide the dough into two pieces, knead well and shape to fit two greased 450-g (1-lb) loaf tins lined with greased greaseproof paper. Cover and leave to prove for 20 minutes.

Make the topping by creaming the butter and sugar and working in the flour until the mixture resembles coarse crumbs. Sprinkle on the loaves and bake for 40 minutes. Cool in the tins for 5 minutes, then turn out and cool on a wire rack.

CARAWAY SEED BREAD

Makes 1 loaf

450 g (1 lb) strong plain white flour
½ tsp salt
2 tsp caraway seeds
15 g (½ oz) fresh yeast or
    7 g (¼ oz) dried yeast
1 tsp brown sugar
300 ml (½ pint) warm water
25 g (1 oz) lard

Sieve the flour and salt into a bowl, and stir in the caraway seeds. Mix the fresh yeast with the sugar and add to the lukewarm water (or sprinkle dried yeast on the water with the sugar and leave until frothy). Rub the lard into the flour until the mixture resembles fine breadcrumbs, then add the yeast liquid. Mix to a dough, knead well, cover and leave to prove for 1 hour.

Heat the oven to 200°C (400°F) mark 6. Knead the dough well again and form into a round loaf. Put on a greased baking sheet, cover and leave to prove for 45 minutes. Bake for 40 minutes. Cool on a wire rack.

This bread tastes particularly good with cheese.

SIMNEL CAKE WITH YEAST

Makes 1

225 g (8 oz) strong plain white flour
½ tsp mixed spice
100 g (4 oz) butter
100 g (4 oz) sugar
15 g (½ oz) fresh yeast or
    7 g (¼ oz) dried yeast
150 ml (¼ pint) warm milk
3 egg yolks
100 g (4 oz) sultanas
100 g (4 oz) currants
double recipe quantity almond paste
    (see page 35) or bought marzipan
2 tbsp apricot jam
a little beaten egg white to glaze

Sieve the flour and spice into a warm bowl and rub in the butter until the mixture resembles fine breadcrumbs. Reserve 1 teaspoon of sugar and stir the rest into the flour. Mix the fresh yeast with the reserved sugar and add to the milk (or sprinkle dried yeast on the milk with the sugar and leave until frothy). Add to the flour with the egg yolks and knead until smooth. Cover and prove for about 1 hour until doubled in size.

Heat the oven to 190°C (375°F) mark 5. Knead the dough again, working in the fruit. Put half the dough into a greased and floured 18-cm (7-inch) diameter cake tin. Take one-third of the almond paste and roll into a circle to fit the tin exactly. Place this on the dough and cover with the remaining

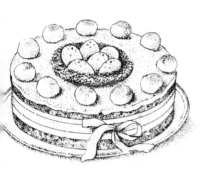

dough. Prove for 30 minutes. Bake for 1½ hours. Leave in the tin for 30 minutes so that the almond paste firms up, and turn out on to a wire rack to cool.

Roll out half the remaining almond paste to fit the top of the cake. Brush the top of the cake with apricot jam and use the marzipan to cover the cake. Make the remaining almond paste into eleven balls and press them round the top of the cake. Brush with a little beaten egg white and put under a hot grill until the almond paste is lightly coloured (this happens very quickly, so keep an eye on the cake all the time). If liked, put a frill or ribbon around the cake, and a decoration of tiny 'eggs' or 'flowers'.

YORKSHIRE OVEN BOTTOM CAKE

Makes 1

100 g (4 oz) risen white bread dough (see page 15)
25 g (1 oz) lard

Heat the oven to 220°C (425°F) mark 7. Cut the lard into six pieces and press into the dough. Fold over and knead the fat into the dough, giving a lumpy appearance. Put on a greased baking sheet and bake for 15 minutes until golden brown. Wrap in a clean tea towel and place on a cushion (this will keep the 'cake' soft and tender). Cut in irregular pieces, split and spread thickly with butter and jam.

Traditionally, this cake was made at the end of the baking day when the loaves were taken out. Before the days of metal trays, the cake was baked directly on the floor of the oven.

SAVOURY BREADS

Yeast dough may be used instead of pastry to form a useful container for savoury ingredients. In Europe, many tempting recipes have been used for centuries to produce handy snack meals which are filling and nourishing.

CHEESE BREAD

Makes two 450-g (1-lb) loaves

450 g (1 lb) strong plain white flour
1 tsp salt
1 tsp mustard powder
¼ tsp pepper
100 g (4 oz) Cheddar cheese, grated
15 g (½ oz) fresh yeast or
   7 g (¼ oz) dried yeast
1 tsp sugar
300 ml (½ pint) warm water

Sieve the flour, salt, mustard and pepper into a bowl. Stir in the cheese, reserving 1 tablespoonful. Mix the fresh yeast with the sugar and add to the lukewarm water (or sprinkle dried yeast on the water with the sugar and leave until frothy). Add to the flour and knead well. Cover and leave to prove for 1 hour.

Heat the oven to 190°C (375°F) mark 5. Knead the dough again and shape to fit two greased 450-g (1-lb) loaf tins. Cover and leave to prove for 20 minutes. Sprinkle with the reserved cheese and bake for 40 minutes. Cool on a wire rack.

CALZONE

Makes 8

450 g (1 lb) strong plain white flour
1 tsp salt
25 g (1 oz) lard
15 g (½ oz) fresh yeast or
   7 g (¼ oz) dried yeast
1 tsp sugar
300 ml (½ pint) warm water
225 g (8 oz) cooked ham
225 g (8 oz) Bel Paese or Gruyère
   cheese
1 tbsp olive oil
salt and pepper

Sieve the flour and salt into a bowl and rub in the lard. Mix the fresh yeast with the sugar and add to the lukewarm water (or sprinkle the dried yeast on the water with the sugar and leave until frothy). Add to the flour and mix to a firm dough. Knead well, cover and leave to prove for 1 hour.

Heat the oven to 220°C (425°F) mark 7. Knead the dough again and divide into eight pieces. Roll out each piece to a 15-cm (6-inch) round. Cut the ham and cheese into eight slices. Place a folded slice of ham and a slice of cheese on half of each round. Sprinkle with olive oil and season well. Fold over the top of the round and press the edges together firmly. Place on a greased baking sheet, cover and leave to prove for 15 minutes. Bake for 20 minutes. Serve warm, if possible with a hot tomato sauce. A sprinkling of Parmesan cheese completes this Italian dish.

NEAPOLITAN PIZZA

Makes 4 pizzas

450 g (1 lb) risen wholemeal dough
(see page 16) or white dough (see
page 15)
olive oil

Filling
350 g (12 oz) mozzarella cheese,
sliced
450 g (1 lb) fresh or canned
tomatoes, sliced
1 tsp pizza herbs (or a mixture of
marjoram, basil and thyme)
a few anchovy fillets
black olives
black pepper

Heat the oven to 230°C (450°F) mark 8.
Roll out the dough into the required
number of pieces: this amount of dough will
make four 18-cm (7-inch) pizzas. Brush
sandwich tins, square or rectangular tins, or
metal pie plates with olive oil, and put in the
dough. Brush again with olive oil.

Cover the dough with alternate layers of
cheese, tomato and seasonings, finishing
with the cheese. Decorate with a lattice of
anchovies and olives. Leave to stand in a
cold place for 30 minutes. Bake for
30 minutes and serve hot.

To obtain the best results, slice the meat,
cheese or vegetables thinly, and season well
with herbs, salt and pepper. Mozzarella
cheese is traditionally used as it melts
quickly and smoothly, but several other
cheeses may be used, such as Cheddar,
Emmenthal, Gruyère and Bel Paese. The
pizza always looks better if the cheese is
sliced rather than grated. For convenience
of serving, it may be easier to make square
or rectangular pizzas.

A pizza may be topped with tomatoes,
herbs, cheese and olives in its most simple
form. More elaborate fillings are made by
adding ham, salami, bacon, fish,
mushrooms or onions, according to taste.
For alternative fillings, see pizza
Francescana and seafood pizza below.

PIZZA FRANCESCANA

Makes 4 pizzas

450 g (1 lb) risen wholemeal dough
(see page 16) or white dough (see
page 15)

Filling
225 g (8 oz) cooked ham
100 g (4 oz) mushrooms, sliced
225 g (8 oz) tomatoes, sliced
salt and pepper
100 g (4 oz) Bel Paese, sliced

Heat the oven to 230°C (450°F) mark 8.
Prepare the dough as for Neapolitan pizza
(see opposite). Cut the ham into strips and
arrange over the dough with the mushrooms
and tomatoes. Season, and finish with the
cheese. Leave to stand in a cold place for
30 minutes. Bake for 30 minutes and serve
while hot.

SEAFOOD PIZZA

Makes 4 pizzas

450 g (1 lb) risen wholemeal dough
(see page 16) or white dough (see
page 15)

Filling
225 g (8 oz) cooked smoked fish
350 g (12 oz) tomatoes, chopped
100 g (4 oz) streaky bacon, diced
100 g (4 oz) peeled prawns
mixed herbs
salt and pepper
100 g (4 oz) mozzarella or other
cheese, sliced

Heat the oven to 230°C (450°F) mark 8.
Prepare the dough as for Neapolitan pizza
(see opposite). Cover the dough with the
smoked fish, tomatoes, bacon and prawns.
Sprinkle with mixed herbs and season to
taste. Finish with the cheese. Leave to stand
in a cold place for 30 minutes. Bake for
30 minutes and serve hot.

ONION TART

Makes 1

225 g (8 oz) risen white dough (see
    page 15) or wholemeal dough (see
    page 16)
225 g (8 oz) onions
50 g (2 oz) butter
15 g (½ oz) plain flour
150 ml (¼ pint) milk
salt and pepper
¼ tsp garlic salt
1 tsp poppy seeds

Heat the oven to 200°C (400°F) mark 6.
Roll out the dough and use to line a greased
20-cm (8-inch) sandwich tin or flan ring.
Cover and leave to prove for 30 minutes.

Peel the onions and slice thinly. Cook
gently in the butter until just soft and
golden brown. Stir in the flour and cook for
1 minute. Gradually add the milk and bring
to the boil. Stir well and simmer for
1 minute. Season with salt, pepper and
garlic salt then cool to lukewarm. Spoon the
onion mixture on to the dough and sprinkle
with poppy seeds. Bake for 30 minutes.
Serve hot.

COULIBIAC

Makes 1

450 g (1 lb) strong plain white flour
15 g (½ oz) fresh yeast or
    7 g (¼ oz) dried yeast
1 tsp sugar
150 ml (¼ pint) warm milk
1 tsp salt
100 g (4 oz) butter, melted
3 eggs, beaten

Filling
450 g (1 lb) cooked smoked haddock
3 hard-boiled eggs
175 g (6 oz) cooked rice
salt and pepper

1 egg yolk to glaze

Sieve the flour into a bowl, then remove
100 g (4 oz) of the flour to a smaller bowl.
Mix the fresh yeast with the sugar and add
to the lukewarm milk (or sprinkle the dried
yeast on the milk with the sugar and leave
until frothy). Add this yeast liquid to the
smaller amount of flour and beat until
smooth. Cover and leave to prove for
30 minutes. Add to the remaining flour
with the salt, butter and eggs, and mix to a
soft dough. Knead well, cover and leave to
prove for 1½ hours.

Heat the oven to 220°C (425°F) mark 7.
Roll the dough into a square 1 cm (½ inch)
thick. Prepare the filling by flaking the fish
and mixing with the chopped eggs and rice;
season well with salt and pepper. Put into
the centre of the dough and fold into a
parcel, sealing the joins with beaten egg
yolk. Place on a greased baking sheet with
the joins underneath. Glaze with egg yolk

and cut two slits in the top. Bake for 45 minutes. Serve hot or cold.

Salmon may be used instead of haddock, and sliced mushrooms may be added to the filling. This is a Russian recipe.

LAHN AJOUN

Makes 12

675 g (1½ lb) risen white bread dough (see page 15)
450 g (1 lb) raw lean lamb
1 large onion, peeled
2 garlic cloves, peeled
1 green pepper, deseeded
4 tbsp fresh parsley, chopped
¼ tsp ground allspice
salt and pepper
225 g (8-oz) can tomatoes

Heat the oven to 220°C (425°F) mark 7. Divide the dough into twelve pieces and roll out each piece thinly to a 15-cm (6-inch) round. Place on greased baking sheets. Mince the lamb, onion, garlic and green pepper together and add the parsley, spice, salt and pepper. Drain the tomatoes and chop the flesh. Add to the lamb and mix well. Divide the mixture between the pieces of dough, and place in the centre of each round, spreading lightly so that the mixture comes to the edges of the dough. Bake for 20 minutes. Roll up and serve hot.

This recipe is from the Middle East.

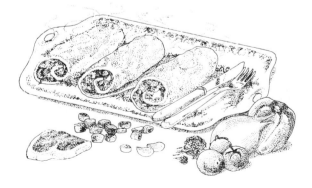

YEAST-FREE BREADS

Since raising agents first appeared in the middle
of the 19th century, the cook has been able to
devise many quickly-made bread substitutes.
The oldest non-yeast breads such as scones and
soft pancakes come from the remote areas of
Scotland, Wales and Ireland, where the griddle
or bakestone was in constant use.

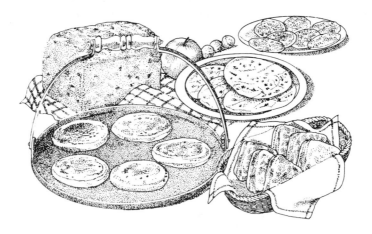

CHAPATTIS

Makes 8

225 g (8 oz) plain wholemeal flour
pinch of salt
25 g (1 oz) butter
175 ml (6 fl oz) water
1 tbsp corn oil

Stir the flour and salt together in a bowl. Rub in the butter until the mixture resembles fine breadcrumbs. Add sufficient water to mix to a stiff dough. Knead on a lightly floured board for 15 minutes. Leave on the board, cover with a bowl and leave to rest for 30 minutes.

Divide the dough into eight pieces and roll out each piece to a 15-cm (6-inch) round. Heat the oil in a frying pan and fry each piece of dough for 3 minutes, turning often to prevent burning.

Serve this Indian bread with curry.

COTTAGE CHEESE TEABREAD

Makes one 900-g (2-lb) loaf

225 g (8 oz) cottage cheese
100 g (4 oz) light soft brown sugar
3 eggs
225 g (8 oz) self-raising flour
1 tsp baking powder
2 sticks celery, finely chopped
50 g (2 oz) shelled walnuts, chopped

Heat the oven to 180°C (350°F) mark 4. Sieve the cottage cheese. Cream the cheese with the sugar and eggs. Sieve the flour and baking powder together and fold into the creamed mixture. Add the celery and walnuts. Put into a greased 900-g (2-lb) loaf tin lined with greased greaseproof paper. Bake for 1 hour. Cool in the tin for 5 minutes, then turn out and cool on a wire rack.

FRUIT BRAN LOAF

Makes one 450-g (1-lb) loaf

100 g (4 oz) mixed dried fruit
75 g (3 oz) All Bran cereal
75 g (3 oz) light soft brown sugar
175 ml (6 fl oz) milk
100 g (4 oz) self-raising flour, sieved

Heat the oven to 180°C (350°F) mark 4. Put the fruit, cereal, sugar and milk into a bowl and leave to soak for 1 hour. Beat in the flour. Pour into a greased 450-g (1-lb) loaf tin lined with greased greaseproof paper and bake for 1 hour. Cool on a wire rack. Slice thickly and spread with butter.

GINGER SULTANA BREAD

Makes one 450-g (1-lb) loaf

175 g (6 oz) plain flour
1½ tsp baking powder
2 tsp ground ginger
75 g (3 oz) butter
75 g (3 oz) light soft brown sugar
75 g (3 oz) sultanas
75 g (3 oz) crystallized or stem
  ginger, chopped
6 tbsp milk

Heat the oven to 180°C (350°F) mark 4. Sieve the flour, baking powder and ground ginger into a bowl. Rub in the butter until the mixture resembles fine breadcrumbs. Stir in the sugar, sultanas and ginger. Add the milk and mix to give a stiff consistency. Put into a greased 450-g (1-lb) loaf tin lined with greased greaseproof paper and bake for 1¼ hours. Cool on a wire rack.

CHEESE AND APPLE BREAD

Makes one 450-g (1-lb) loaf

225 g (8 oz) self-raising flour
½ tsp salt
pinch of pepper
25 g (1 oz) butter or margarine
1 eating apple
100 g (4 oz) Cheddar cheese, grated
50 g (2 oz) shelled walnuts, chopped
1 egg
150 ml (¼ pint) milk

Heat the oven to 190°C (375°F) mark 5. Sieve the flour, salt and pepper into a bowl. Rub in the fat until the mixture resembles fine breadcrumbs. Peel, core and finely chop the apple and add to the dry ingredients with the cheese and walnuts. Mix with the beaten egg and milk. Put into a greased 450-g (1-lb) loaf tin lined with greased greaseproof paper and bake for 45 minutes. Cool on a wire rack. Serve sliced and buttered with salad.

POPOVERS

Makes 8

100 g (4 oz) plain flour
pinch of salt
2 eggs
200 ml (7 fl oz) milk
1 tbsp melted butter

Heat the oven to 230°C (450°F) mark 8. Sieve the flour and salt into a bowl. Beat the eggs and milk together and beat into the flour with the butter. Beat thoroughly until smooth and then pour into hot, greased individual deep patty tins or Yorkshire pudding tins. Bake for 20 minutes, then reduce the temperature to 180°C (350°F) mark 4 and continue baking for 10 minutes or until very crisp. Serve hot.

BOSTON BROWN BREAD

Makes 2 loaves

100 g (4 oz) rye flour
100 g (4 oz) cornmeal
100 g (4 oz) plain wholemeal flour
1 tsp salt
1 tsp bicarbonate of soda
175 ml (6 oz) black treacle
450 ml (¾ pint) buttermilk
100 g (4 oz) chopped raisins
    (optional)

This bread is traditionally steamed in cylindrical cans from which the tops and bottoms have been removed (coffee or other food cans may be used). If these cans are not available, use stone jam jars, or pudding basins.

Mix together the flours, salt and soda and work in the treacle, milk and raisins. Beat well and fill the greased cans three-quarters full. Cover firmly with greased paper and foil. Put into a pan of boiling water to come half-way up the cans. Cover and steam for 3 hours, topping up the pan with boiling water as necessary.

This bread is the traditional accompaniment to baked beans, and is served hot with butter. The raisins may be omitted.

ELY DOUGH CAKE

Makes one 900-g (2-lb) loaf

225 g (8 oz) mixed dried fruit
200 ml (8 fl oz) cold strong tea
    (without milk)
350 g (12 oz) self-raising flour,
    sieved
175 g (6 oz) dark soft brown sugar
2 eggs, beaten
½ tsp mixed spice
pinch of salt
1 tbsp caster sugar

Heat the oven to 180°C (350°F) mark 4. Put the fruit into a large bowl and pour on the tea. Leave to stand overnight. Beat in the flour, sugar, eggs, spice and salt until well mixed. Put into a well greased 900-g (2-lb) loaf tin, and bake for 1 hour. Brush the surface with the sugar dissolved in 2 tablespoons water. Continue baking for 30 minutes then turn out and cool on a wire rack. Serve sliced with butter.

BAKING POWDER BREAD

Makes two 450-g (1-lb) loaves

450 g (1 lb) plain flour
1 tbsp baking powder
pinch of salt
300 ml (½ pint) milk and water,
  mixed

Heat the oven to 220°C (425°F) mark 7. Sieve the flour, baking powder and salt into a bowl. Add the liquid and mix to a firm dough, but do not knead. Shape to fit two greased 450-g (1-lb) loaf tins and brush the tops with a little milk. Bake for 25 minutes. Cool on a wire rack. Eat freshly baked as this bread does not keep.

WHOLEMEAL SODA BREAD

Makes 1 loaf

350 g (12 oz) plain wholemeal flour
225 g (8 oz) plain white flour
1 tsp bicarbonate of soda
2 tsp cream of tartar
2 tsp salt
300 ml (½ pint) milk
4 tbsp water

Heat the oven to 220°C (425°F) mark 7. Put the wholemeal flour into a bowl. Sieve in the white flour, soda, cream of tartar and salt. Mix to a soft dough with the milk and water. Put on to a floured board and knead lightly. Shape into a round about 5 cm (2 inches) thick. Place on a floured baking sheet and with a sharp knife, cut a deep cross on the dough. Sprinkle with a little flour and bake for 25 minutes. Cool on a wire rack. Eat while fresh.

IRISH BOXTY BREAD

Makes 2 loaves

225 g (8 oz) raw potatoes
225 g (8 oz) boiled potatoes
225 g (8 oz) plain white flour,
  sieved
½ tsp salt
pinch of pepper
50 g (2 oz) butter or bacon fat,
  melted

Heat the oven to 150°C (300°F) mark 2. Peel the raw potatoes and grate them coarsely. Mash the boiled potatoes and work in the raw potatoes, flour, salt, pepper and melted fat, and mix well but do not knead. Divide the dough into two pieces, press out each piece into a flat round and place on a greased baking sheet. Mark each piece into quarters but do not cut through. Bake for 40 minutes. While hot, break into quarters and serve with butter.

SELF-RAISING FLOUR BREAD

Makes 1 loaf

450 g (1 lb) self-raising flour
1 tsp salt
25 g (1 oz) butter
300 ml (½ pint) milk and water,
    mixed

Heat the oven to 220°C (425°F) mark 7. Sieve the flour and salt into a bowl. Rub in the butter until the mixture resembles fine breadcrumbs. Mix to a firm dough with the milk and water, and knead until smooth. Form into a round loaf and place on a greased baking sheet. Bake for 35 minutes. Cool on a wire rack. Eat freshly baked as this bread does not keep.

YOGHURT BREAD

Makes one 450-g (1-lb) loaf

450 g (1 lb) plain wholemeal flour
2 tsp baking powder
2 tsp light soft brown sugar
1 tsp salt
1 tbsp freshly chopped herbs
    (optional)
50 ml (¼ pint) natural yoghurt
50 ml (¼ pint) water

Heat the oven to 220°C (425°F) mark 7. Mix the flour, baking powder, sugar and salt together in a bowl. Add the yoghurt and sufficient water to make a soft dough. Knead well and shape to fit a greased 450 g (1 lb) loaf tin. Bake for 45 minutes. Cool on a wire rack.

This bread is particularly good if 1 tablespoon of freshly chopped herbs are added to the dry ingredients. Serve with cheese or salads.

AMERICAN CORNBREAD

Makes 1 'loaf'

90 g (4 oz) plain flour
90 g (4 oz) cornmeal
1 tsp baking powder
1 tsp sugar
2 tsp salt
1 egg
50 ml (8 fl oz) milk
1 tbsp melted butter

Heat the oven to 200°C (400°F) mark 6. Mix the flour, cornmeal, baking powder, sugar and salt together in a bowl. Beat the egg and milk together and add to the flour with the butter. Pour into a greased rectangular tin 30 x 20 cm (12 x 8 inches). Bake for 35 minutes, and serve hot. Left-over cornbread may be split and toasted.

CHERRY AND BANANA LOAF

Makes one 900-g (2-lb) loaf

225 g (8 oz) self-raising flour
pinch of salt
175 g (6 oz) light soft brown sugar
100 g (4 oz) soft tub margarine
2 eggs, beaten
100 g (4 oz) glacé cherries, chopped
2 ripe bananas, mashed

Heat the oven to 160°C (325°F) mark 3. Sieve the flour and salt into a bowl and stir in the sugar. Add the margarine, beaten eggs, chopped cherries and mashed bananas. Beat hard for about 2 minutes until well mixed. Put into a greased 900-g (2-lb) loaf tin lined with greased greaseproof paper and bake for 1½ hours. Cool on a wire rack.

NUT BREAD

Makes one 450-g (1-lb) loaf

175 g (6 oz) self-raising flour
pinch of salt
50 g (2 oz) porridge oats
100 g (4 oz) light soft brown sugar
100 g (4 oz) butter
75 g (3 oz) shelled walnuts, chopped
2 eggs, beaten
4 tbsp milk

Heat the oven to 180°C (350°F) mark 4. Sieve the flour and salt into a bowl. Stir in the oats and sugar. Rub in the butter until the mixture resembles fine breadcrumbs then stir in the walnuts. Add the beaten eggs and milk, and mix well.

Put into a greased 450-g (1-lb) loaf tin lined with greased greaseproof paper and bake for 1¼ hours. Turn out and cool on a wire rack.

DATE BREAD

Makes one 900-g (2-lb) loaf

225 g (8 oz) stoned dates
175 g (6 fl oz) cold tea, without milk
225 g (8 oz) plain wholemeal flour
175 g (6 oz) light soft brown sugar
4 tsp baking powder
1 tsp mixed spice
1 egg, beaten
25 g (1 oz) demerara sugar

Heat the oven to 180°C (350°F) mark 4. Chop the dates and place in a bowl. Pour on the tea and leave to stand for 2 hours. In a separate bowl, mix the flour, sugar, baking powder and spice together. Add the dates and their soaking liquid, and the egg. Mix well. Put into a greased 900-g (2-lb) loaf tin lined with greased greaseproof paper. Sprinkle with demerara sugar and bake for 1¼ hours. Cool in the tin for 5 minutes, then turn out and cool on a wire rack.

SUSSEX HONEY BREAD

Makes one 450-g (1-lb) loaf

175 g (6 oz) plain flour
75 g (3 oz) demerara sugar
1 tsp bicarbonate of soda
1 tsp mixed spice
pinch of salt
25 g (1 oz) margarine
1 egg
75 g (3 oz) clear honey
150 ml (¼ pint) water
50 g (2 oz) currants or sultanas

Heat the oven to 180°C (350°F) mark 4. Sieve the flour into a bowl. Stir in the sugar, soda, spice and salt then rub in the margarine. Beat the egg and honey together with the water, then beat into the dry ingredients followed by the currants or sultanas. Put into a greased 450-g (1-lb) loaf tin lined with greased greaseproof paper and bake for 1 hour. Cool on a wire rack.

SULTANA MALT BREAD

Makes one 900-g (2-lb) loaf

450 g (1 lb) self-raising flour
2 tsp bicarbonate of soda
pinch of salt
300 ml (½ pint) milk
4 tbsp malt extract
4 tbsp golden syrup
225 g (8 oz) sultanas
2 eggs, beaten

Heat the oven to 180°C (350°F) mark 4. Sieve the flour, soda and salt into a bowl. Heat the milk with the malt and syrup until lukewarm. Add to the flour and mix well. Add the sultanas and beat well. Put into a greased 900-g (2-lb) loaf tin lined with greased greaseproof paper and bake for 1¼ hours. Cool on a wire rack.

OATMEAL BREAD

Makes one 900-g (2-lb) loaf

225 g (8 oz) plain wholemeal flour
175 g (6 oz) coarse oatmeal
2 tsp cream of tartar
1 tsp bicarbonate of soda
1 tsp salt
300 ml (½ pint) milk and water,
* mixed*

Heat the oven to 220°C (425°F) mark 7. Mix the flour, oatmeal, cream of tartar, soda and salt together in a bowl. Add sufficient milk and water to make a firm dough. Shape to fit a greased 900-g (2-lb) loaf tin. Bake for 25 minutes. Cool on a wire rack.

TREACLE LOAF

Makes one 900-g (2-lb) loaf

225 g (8 oz) plain wholemeal flour
225 g (8 oz) plain white flour,
   sieved
100 g (4 oz) sugar
150 g (5 oz) seedless raisins
25 g (1 oz) chopped mixed nuts
175 g (6 oz) black treacle
300 ml (½ pint) milk
½ tsp bicarbonate of soda
1 egg, beaten

Mix the flours, sugar, raisins and nuts together in a bowl. Heat the treacle and milk together until lukewarm. Add the soda and pour on to the dry ingredients. Add the egg and beat well. Put into a greased 900-g (2-lb) loaf tin lined with greased greaseproof paper and bake for 1½ hours. Cool on a wire rack.

SODA BREAD

Makes 1 loaf

450 g (1 lb) plain white flour
1 tsp salt
½ tsp bicarbonate of soda
½ tsp cream of tartar
25 g (1 oz) butter
300 ml (½ pint) buttermilk or sour
   milk

Heat the oven to 220°C (425°F) mark 7. Sieve the flour, salt, soda and cream of tartar into a bowl. Rub in the butter, add the milk and mix to form a soft dough. Put on to a floured board and knead lightly. Shape into a round about 5 cm (2 inches) thick. Place on a floured baking sheet and with a sharp knife, cut a deep cross on the dough. Sprinkle with a little flour and bake for 25 minutes. Cool on a wire rack. Eat while fresh.

WAFFLES

Makes 8

175 g (6 oz) plain flour
pinch of salt
3 tsp baking powder
25 g (1 oz) caster sugar
2 eggs
300 ml (½ pint) milk
50 g (2 oz) butter, melted

Sieve the flour, salt and baking powder into a bowl. Stir in the sugar. Separate the eggs and mix the egg yolks with the milk. Gradually add to the flour with the cooled butter, beating well. Whisk the egg whites to stiff peaks and fold into the batter.

Heat a waffle-iron and brush with a little melted butter. Spoon a little batter into the

waffle iron, close it and cook for
1–2 minutes on each side until golden
brown. Serve hot with honey or syrup.

If a waffle iron is not available, fry
tablespoons of the batter in a lightly greased
frying pan, cooking on each side until
golden brown.

SPICED HONEY LOAF

Makes one 900-g (2-lb) loaf

300 g (10 oz) plain flour
pinch of salt
½ tsp bicarbonate of soda
½ tsp baking powder
½ tsp mixed spice
½ tsp ground ginger
½ tsp ground cinnamon
50 g (2 oz) chopped mixed peel
50 g (5 oz) honey
50 g (5 oz) demerara sugar
50 g (2 oz) butter or margarine
1 egg
150 ml (¼ pint) milk
15 g (½ oz) flaked almonds

Heat the oven to 180°C (350°F) mark 4.
Sieve the flour, salt, soda, baking powder
and spices into a bowl and add the peel.
Heat the honey, sugar and fat together until
the fat has just melted, and leave to cool.
Whisk the egg and milk together and beat
into the honey mixture. Add to the flour
and beat well. Put into a greased 900-g
(2 lb) loaf tin lined with greased greaseproof
paper. Sprinkle with flaked almonds and
bake for 1½ hours. Cool on a wire rack.

PIKELETS

225 g (8 oz) plain flour
pinch of salt
50 g (2 oz) caster sugar
150 ml (¼ pint) milk
½ tsp bicarbonate of soda
1 tbsp boiling water

Sieve the flour and salt into a bowl and stir
in the sugar. Beat in the milk. Dissolve the
soda in the boiling water and beat into the
batter. Drop tablespoons of the batter on to
a hot griddle or thick frying pan. Cook until
golden brown underneath, turn over and
continue cooking until golden on the
underside. Eat hot with butter.

EMERGENCY BREAKFAST ROLLS

Makes 18

450 g (1 lb) plain flour
2 tsp baking powder
100 g (4 oz) butter
40 g (1½ oz) caster sugar
300 ml (½ pint) milk

Heat the oven to 220°C (425°F) mark 7. Sieve the flour and baking powder into a bowl. Rub in the butter until the mixture resembles fine breadcrumbs. Stir in the sugar and work in the milk to make a soft dough. Divide the mixture into 18 pieces, and shape into rolls. Put on a greased baking sheet, allowing room for expansion. Bake for 15 minutes. Cool on a wire rack. Eat freshly baked with marmalade, jam or honey.

OATCAKES

Makes 8–10

175 g (6 oz) fine oatmeal
50 g (2 oz) plain flour
pinch of salt
25 g (1 oz) lard or dripping, melted
boiling water

Heat the oven to 180°C (350°F) mark 4. Mix the oatmeal, flour and salt together in a bowl. Add the melted fat and just enough boiling water to form a stiff dough. Roll out thinly on a board sprinkled with oatmeal. Cut into triangles or 7.5-cm (3-inch) rounds. Place on a greased baking sheet and bake for 30 minutes, or cook on a lightly greased griddle or thick frying pan over a gentle heat. Cool on a wire rack and, when cold, store in an airtight container.

MEXICAN TORTILLAS

Makes 4

225 g (8 oz) cornmeal
225 g (8 oz) plain flour, sieved
1 tsp salt
25 g (1 oz) lard or margarine
300 ml (½ pint) warm water

Mix the cornmeal, flour and salt together in a bowl. Rub in the fat until the mixture resembles fine breadcrumbs. Add sufficient lukewarm water to mix to a dough and knead until smooth. Divide the dough into four pieces and roll into balls; cover and leave to stand for 1 hour.

Roll out each ball on a lightly floured

board to make 25-cm (10-inch) rounds. Cook each round of dough on a well greased griddle, or thick frying pan, until lightly browned on each side.

This bread is sometimes used as a plate on which meat and bean mixtures may be served, or it can be wrapped around a mixture. The uncooked tortilla may be stuffed, fried and served with sauce.

APPLE NUT BREAD

Makes one 900-g (2-lb) loaf

225 g (8 oz) self-raising flour
1 tsp baking powder
½ tsp ground cinnamon
pinch of ground nutmeg
50 g (2 oz) shelled walnuts, finely chopped
75 g (3 oz) butter
125 g (5 oz) light soft brown sugar
2 eggs
2 tbsp milk
40 g (1½ oz) seedless raisins
1 cooking apple
100 g (4 oz) icing sugar
a little warm water

Heat the oven to 180°C (350°F) mark 4. Sieve together the flour, baking powder and spices and stir in the chopped walnuts. Cream the butter and sugar until light and fluffy. Beat the eggs and milk together. Add the dry ingredients to the creamed mixture, alternating with the eggs. Stir in the raisins. Peel, core and dice the apple, and stir into the cake mixture.

Put into a greased 900-g (2-lb) loaf tin lined with greased greaseproof paper and bake for 1 hour. Cool on a wire rack and ice with the sieved icing sugar mixed with a little warm water.

PINEAPPLE BREAD

Makes one 900-g (2-lb) loaf

225-g (8-oz) can pineapple in
  natural juice
50 g (2 oz) shelled walnuts
100 g (4 oz) butter
50 g (2 oz) caster sugar
3 tbsp black treacle
1 egg, beaten
350 g (12 oz) self-raising flour,
  sieved
175 g (6 oz) icing sugar, sieved

Heat the oven to 180°C (350°F) mark 4.
Drain the pineapple and reserve the juice.
Chop the pineapple coarsely, and the
walnuts finely. Cream the butter, sugar and
treacle together until light and fluffy.
Gradually beat the egg into the creamed
mixture with a little of the flour to prevent
curdling. Fold in the remaining flour with
the chopped pineapple, walnuts, and
4 tablespoons of the pineapple juice.

Put into a greased 900-g (2-lb) loaf tin
lined with greased greaseproof paper and
bake for 1 hour. Cool on a wire rack and ice
with the icing sugar mixed with
2 tablespoons pineapple juice.

DEVONSHIRE CIDER BREAD

Makes one 900-g (2-lb) loaf

350 g (12 oz) mixed dried fruit
300 ml (½ pint) sweet cider
300 g (10 oz) self-raising flour
175 g (6 oz) light soft brown sugar
50 g (2 oz) shelled walnuts, chopped
2 eggs, beaten

Heat the oven to 180°C (350°F) mark 4. Put
the dried fruit into a bowl and pour on the
cider. Cover and leave to stand for
12 hours. Transfer to a saucepan and bring
to the boil. Remove from the heat and leave
to cool.

Sieve the flour into a bowl and stir in the
sugar and walnuts. Beat in the fruit mixture
and eggs. Put into a greased 900-g (2-lb) loaf
tin lined with greased greaseproof paper and
bake for 30 minutes. Reduce the
temperature to 160°C (325°F) mark 3 and
continue baking for 45 minutes. Cool on a
wire rack.

BANANA BREAD

Makes one 900-g (2-lb) loaf

225 g (8 oz) self-raising flour
½ tsp salt
75 g (3 oz) margarine
150 g (5 oz) light soft brown sugar
2 eggs
1 tbsp golden syrup, warmed
3 medium bananas
50 g (2 oz) seedless raisins
40 g (1½ oz) chopped mixed nuts

Heat the oven to 180°C (350°F) mark 4. Sieve the flour and salt together and rub in the margarine until the mixture resembles fine breadcrumbs. Stir in the sugar. Beat the eggs and add to the mixture with the warm syrup. Mash the bananas and work into the flour mixture followed by the raisins and the nuts.

Put into a well-greased 900-g (2-lb) loaf tin and bake for 1½ hours. Cool on a wire rack. If possible, store in an airtight container or wrap in foil for a day or two before eating, as this improves the flavour.

WHOLEMEAL HERB ROUND

Makes 1 loaf

225 g (8 oz) plain wholemeal flour
1 tsp cream of tartar
½ tsp bicarbonate of soda
½ tsp salt
large pinch of ground pepper
50 g (2 oz) butter or margarine
1 tsp dried mixed herbs
150 ml (¼ pint) natural yoghurt
milk to glaze

Heat the oven to 220°C (425°F) mark 7. Mix the flour, cream of tartar, soda, salt and pepper together in a bowl. Rub the fat into the flour until the mixture resembles fine breadcrumbs, then stir in the herbs. Add the yoghurt and work to a soft dough, kneading until smooth.

Shape the dough into a round and press out until 1 cm (½ inch) thick. Place on a greased baking sheet and score with a sharp knife into six portions. Brush with milk and bake for 25 minutes. Serve freshly baked with cheese or soup.

BAKING POWDER TEACAKES

Makes 6

350 g (12 oz) plain flour
1½ tsp baking powder
pinch of salt
75 g (3 oz) butter
50 g (2 oz) sugar
50 g (2 oz) sultanas
25 g (1 oz) chopped mixed peel
1 egg, beaten
175 ml (7 fl oz) milk

Heat the oven to 220°C (425°F) mark 7. Sieve the flour, baking powder and salt into a bowl. Rub in the butter until the mixture resembles fine breadcrumbs, then stir in the sugar, sultanas and peel. Add the egg and sufficient milk to mix to a soft dough. Divide the mixture into six pieces and shape into flat round cakes. Put on a greased baking sheet. Bake for 20 minutes. Cool on a wire rack.

AFTERNOON TEA SCONES

Makes 12

225 g (8 oz) plain flour
1 tsp cream of tartar
½ tsp bicarbonate of soda
½ tsp salt
50 g (2 oz) butter or margarine
25 g (1 oz) caster sugar
about 150 ml (¼ pint) milk
beaten egg or milk to glaze

Heat the oven to 220°C (425°F) mark 7. Sieve the flour, cream of tartar, soda and salt into a bowl. Rub in the fat until the mixture resembles fine breadcrumbs, then stir in the sugar. Add sufficient milk to mix to a soft dough. Knead very lightly on a floured board and roll out to 2 cm (¾ inch) thick. Cut into rounds 4–5 cm (1½–2 inches) across and place close together on a greased baking sheet. Brush with beaten egg or milk. Bake for 15 minutes. Cool on a wire rack.

To make fruit scones add 100 g (4 oz) mixed dried fruit to the dry ingredients.

YOGHURT DROP SCONES

75 g (3 oz) self-raising flour
pinch of salt
150 ml (¼ pint) natural yoghurt
1 egg

Sieve the flour and salt into a bowl. Add the yoghurt and egg, and mix to form a thick creamy batter. Drop tablespoons of the batter on to a greased thick frying pan or griddle, and cook over a moderate heat unti the surface bubbles. Turn over and cook until the undersides are golden. Wrap in a clean tea-towel, so that they remain soft as they cool. Serve warm with butter and jam or honey.

WELSH BAKESTONE CAKES

Makes 15

225 g (8 oz) self-raising flour
50 g (2 oz) lard
25 g (1 oz) margarine
40 g (1½ oz) sugar
75 g (3 oz) currants
pinch of ground nutmeg

Sieve the flour into a bowl. Rub in the lard and margarine until the mixture resembles fine breadcrumbs then stir in the sugar, currants, and the nutmeg. Add sufficient cold water to mix to a soft dough. Roll out on a floured board to a thickness of 2.5 cm (1 inch) and cut into 5-cm (2-inch) rounds. Dredge a thick frying pan or griddle with flour, heat and cook the cakes on one side until golden brown. Turn over and continue cooking until the second side is golden brown. Serve freshly cooked.

TREACLE DROP SCONES

Makes 15

225 g (8 oz) self-raising flour
½ tsp salt
½ tsp ground nutmeg
2 tsp caster sugar
1 egg
2 tbsp black treacle
300 ml (½ pint) milk
75 g (3 oz) seedless raisins

Sieve the flour, salt and nutmeg into a bowl then stir in the sugar. Beat the egg with the treacle and milk and gradually beat into the flour to give a creamy batter. Drop tablespoons of the batter on to a greased griddle or thick frying pan, and put five or six raisins on each one. When the batter is set and the scones have risen, turn and cook the other side until golden brown.

Wrap the warm scones in a clean tea-towel so that they remain soft as they cool. Serve with butter. These are best eaten fresh.

DROP SCONES

Makes 12

225 g (8 oz) plain flour
1 tsp cream of tartar
½ tsp bicarbonate of soda
½ tsp salt
25 g (1 oz) caster sugar
1 egg
250 ml (8 fl oz) milk
1 tbsp oil

Sieve the flour, cream of tartar, soda and salt into a bowl, then stir in the sugar. Gradually beat in the egg, milk and oil to make a thick creamy batter. Lightly grease a heavy frying pan or griddle. Drop tablespoons of the batter on to the griddle and cook over a moderate heat until the surface bubbles. Turn over and continue to cook until golden on the underside. Wrap the warm scones in a clean tea-towel while the rest of the batter is cooking, so that the scones remain tender. Best eaten fresh.

IRISH BANNOCK

Makes 1

350 g (12 oz) plain flour
1 tsp bicarbonate of soda
1 tsp cream of tartar
25 g (1 oz) caster sugar
100 g (4 oz) sultanas
300 ml (½ pint) buttermilk or sour
    milk
caster sugar for dredging

Heat the oven to 200°C (400°F) mark 6. Sieve the flour, soda and cream of tartar into a bowl, then stir in the sugar and sultanas. Add the milk and mix to form a soft dough. Place in a well greased 18-cm (7-inch) sandwich tin, spreading lightly to cover the surface. Bake for 30 minutes. Remove from the tin and sprinkle the surface with a little extra caster sugar. Wrap the bannock in a clean teacloth (so that the surface remains soft) and leave on a wire rack to cool. Serve sliced with butter.

BARLEY BANNOCKS

450 g (1 lb) barley meal
100 g (4 oz) plain flour
2 tsp cream of tartar
½ tsp salt
2 tsp bicarbonate of soda
350 ml (12 fl oz) buttermilk

Mix the barley meal, flour, cream of tartar and salt together in a bowl. Stir the soda into the milk and pour into the dry ingredients. Work to a soft dough and roll out on a floured board to 1 cm (½ inch) thick. Cut into rounds the size of a small meat plate. Cook on a hot floured griddle or thick frying pan until golden brown. Turn over and cook until the underside is golden. Serve warm or cold, but fresh.

BRAN SCONES

Makes 18

350 g (12 oz) plain wholemeal flour
75 g (3 oz) bran
1 tbsp baking powder
pinch of salt
75 g (3 oz) butter or margarine
75 g (3 oz) light soft brown sugar
1 egg, beaten
300 ml (½ pint) milk

Heat the oven to 220°C (425°F) mark 7. Mix the flour, bran, baking powder and salt together in a bowl. Rub in the fat until the mixture resembles fine breadcrumbs, then stir in the sugar. Add the egg and sufficient milk to mix to a soft dough.

Knead very lightly on a floured board and roll out lightly to 2 cm (¾ inch) thick. Cut into rounds 2.5–5 cm (1–2 inches) across and place close together on a greased baking sheet. Bake for 15 minutes. Cool on a wire rack.

CHEESE SCONES

Makes 15

225 g (8 oz) self-raising flour
1 tsp mustard powder
½ tsp salt
pinch of pepper
50 g (2 oz) butter
100 g (4 oz) Cheddar cheese, grated
1 egg, beaten
4 tbsp milk
beaten egg or milk to glaze

Heat the oven to 200°C (400°F) mark 6. Sieve the flour, mustard, salt and pepper into a bowl. Rub in the butter until the mixture resembles fine breadcrumbs then stir in 75 g (3 oz) of the cheese. Add the egg and sufficient milk to mix to a soft dough. Knead very lightly on a floured board and roll out to 2 cm (¾ inch) thick. Cut into rounds 4–5 cm (1½–2 inches) across and place close together on a greased baking sheet. Brush with beaten egg or milk and sprinkle with the remaining cheese. Bake for 20 minutes. Cool on a wire rack.

WHOLEMEAL FRUIT SCONES

Makes 18

225 g (8 oz) plain wholemeal flour
1 tbsp baking powder
1 tsp mixed spice
100 g (4 oz) butter or margarine
25 g (1 oz) light soft brown sugar
100 g (4 oz) mixed dried fruit
1 egg, beaten
150 ml (¼ pint) milk

Heat the oven to 220°C (425°F) mark 7. Mix the flour, baking powder and spice together in a bowl. Rub in the fat until the mixture resembles fine breadcrumbs then stir in the sugar and fruit. Add the egg and sufficient milk to mix to a soft dough. Knead lightly on a lightly floured board and roll out to 2 cm (¾ inch) thick. Cut into rounds 4–5 cm (1½–2 inches) across and place close together on a greased baking sheet. Bake for 15 minutes and cool on a wire rack.

COTTAGE CHEESE DROP SCONES

Makes 10

50 g (2 oz) self-raising flour
100 g (4 oz) cottage cheese
1 tbsp melted butter
2 eggs
1 tbsp milk

Sieve the flour into a bowl. Mix the cottage cheese and butter together and gradually work in the flour, beaten eggs and milk to make a smooth, thick batter. Drop tablespoons of the batter on to a greased thick frying pan or griddle, and cook over a moderate heat until the surface bubbles. Turn over and cook until the undersides are golden brown. Wrap in a clean tea-towel, so that they remain soft. Serve warm with honey or jam, or with crisp bacon.

These drop scones are particularly useful for those who do not wish to use a lot of flour for dietary reasons.

AMERICAN MUFFINS

Makes 15–18

225 g (8 oz) self-raising flour
1 tsp baking powder
pinch of salt
50 g (2 oz) butter or margarine
1 egg
250 ml (8 fl oz) milk

Heat the oven to 220°C (425°F) mark 7.
Sieve the flour, baking powder and salt into
a bowl and rub in the fat until the mixture
resembles fine breadcrumbs. Add the egg
and milk and beat well. Pour into 15–18
greased deep patty tins and bake for
15 minutes. Cool on a wire rack. Serve split
and buttered, either warm or cold.

These muffins may be flavoured with a little
crisply-grilled and chopped bacon, chopped
cooked ham, grated cheese, or dried fruit
and/or nuts.

IRISH WHOLEMEAL GINGERBREAD

100 g (4 oz) plain white flour,
   sieved
100 g (4 oz) plain wholemeal flour
pinch of salt
1 tsp mixed spice
3 tsp ground ginger
40 g (1½ oz) demerara sugar
40 g (1½ oz) chopped mixed peel
40 g (1½ oz) sultanas
100 g (4 oz) butter or margarine
100 g (4 oz) golden syrup
100 g (4 oz) black treacle
1 egg
150 ml (¼ pint) milk
1 tsp bicarbonate soda
25 g (1 oz) split blanched almonds

Heat the oven to 180°C (350°F) mark 4.
Mix together the white and wholemeal
flours, salt, spice, ginger, sugar, peel and
sultanas. Heat the fat, syrup and treacle
together until the fat has melted. Pour into
the dry ingredients, mix well, then beat in
the egg. Warm the milk and stir in the soda.
Add to the mixture and beat to a smooth
batter. Put into a greased 23 x 15 cm
(9 x 6 inch) tin lined with greased
greaseproof paper. Scatter the blanched
almonds on top.
   Bake for 45 minutes and cool in the tin
before turning out. Keep in an airtight
container for two or three days before using.

WHAT IS THE WI ?

If you have enjoyed this book, the chances are that you would enjoy belonging to the largest women's organisation in the country — the Women's Institutes.

We are friendly, go-ahead, like-minded women, who derive enormous satisfaction from all the movement has to offer. This list is long — you can make new friends, have fun and companionship, visit new places, develop new skills, take part in community services, fight local campaigns, become a WI market producer, and play an active role in an organisation which has a national voice.

The WI is the only women's organisation in the country which owns an adult education establishment. At Denman College, you can take a course in anything from car maintenance to paper sculpture, from book binding to yoga, or cordon bleu cookery to fly-fishing.

All you need to do to join is write to us here at the **National Federation of Women's Institutes, 39 Eccleston Street, London SW1W 9NT**, or telephone 01-730 7212, and we will put you in touch with WIs in your immediate locality. We hope to hear from you.

ABOUT THE AUTHOR

Mary Norwak has written over 70 books, including *The Farmhouse Kitchen*, *English Puddings* and more than a dozen titles on freezer cookery. She gives cookery demonstrations to many different groups. A member of the WI for over 25 years, Mary Norwak belongs to Cley WI and serves on the Executive Committee of the Norfolk Federation of Women's Institutes.

INDEX